"In this book, Kevin Giles shows how biblical often been misinterpreted and used to perpe Christians globally and especially in the dev descriptive statistics and vivid retelling of real-time experiences in Australia and in Africa, where he ministered with his wife Lynley, Kevin reveals how male headship can undermine the dignity of women and lead to their abuse. I highly recommend this book for use all over the world."

—**Diphus Chemorion**, Associate Professor and Dean of Faculty of Theology, St. Paul's University, Limuru, Kenya

"Kevin Giles had clear reasons for writing this book. Married to a marriage counselor and active as a theologian, his concern has long been that our understanding of good theology encourages us into healthy relationships. But the converse is also true: bad or distorted theology can play into abusive relationships, and that is his subject here. Those of us who have worked long in this field know how difficult it is to bring the evidence to a wider Christian public. Yet it has to be done. Here it is done with care, biblical acumen, and compassion. I hope the book will become a seminary text, for the next generation of pastors, lay leaders, and counselors who must be given the biblical tools to help to turn the tide, and bring redemptive hope into many more intimate relationships."

—**Elaine Storkey**, Newnham College, Cambridge University, author of *Scars Across Humanity: Understanding and Overcoming Violence Against Women*

"Pastor and theologian Kevin Giles reveals how belief in the unbiblical doctrine of male headship often leads to physical and sexual abuse in the church and the home. Like a doctor who takes no pleasure in telling a critically ill patient of his diagnosis, Kevin shows the horrific outcomes of a belief in male headship and inherent male authority, two concepts that are contradictory to the teachings of Christ and the Scriptures. Every Christian in a position of influence or leadership should read this book before the next physical or sexual abuse scandal rocks your denomination like it did mine."

—**Wade Burleson**, Pastor, Southern Baptist Convention, USA, author of *Fraudulent Authority*

"This small book is packed full of critical information, important truths, needed challenges, and helpful correctives as it relates to how concerned Christians should think about the topic of domestic abuse. It is a must-have for clergy and seminary students."

—**Nancy Nason-Clark**, Professor Emerita, Department of Sociology,
University of New Brunswick

"A nation, church, and family can be measured by its treatment of women. Despite gains made worldwide, women still encounter tragic levels of abuse even in Christian communities. With a long history of advancing the biblical basis for women's equal leadership, Kevin Giles turns his incisive mind to the #MeToo and #ChurchToo crisis. Given that more than 80 percent of the world follow a faith tradition—most of which support male-authority, Giles critiques those with the greatest influence—male religious leaders. Those who speak for God require the greatest accountability. It is to them that this book is addressed. It is to all of us, that this book informs."

—**Mimi Haddad**, President, CBE International

"I warmly commend this book. I invited Kevin and Lynley Giles to Kenya and Uganda in 2018 to speak at conferences for clergy and their wives on marriage in a context where domestic abuse and violence is common, and sadly all too often in clergy homes. From the Scriptures, and from their over fifty years of marriage they ministered powerfully to those present. What they said and how they related to each other as equal partners in their marriage opened up possibilities hitherto not envisaged by so many clergy couples. What was so amazing was the number of men who recognized that their selfishness and determination to have their own way had resulted in a very unhappy marriage and it was they who needed to change for marital love to flourish. In his discussion of the abuse of women in the developing world, Kevin recounts this story."

—**Patti Ricotta**, President and Co-Founder, Life Together International

"I commend Kevin Giles for producing a well-researched and thoughtful book on how Christian churches need to recognize domestic and family violence and respond and refer appropriately. The history of discrimination against women in the churches has created generations of women and girls who have come to believe that they are beneath and inferior to men and as a consequence have accepted their marginalization and abuse in one way or another. Kevin Giles forcefully argues that church leaders today must take responsibility for this diminishment of women that all too often has allowed, if not encouraged, domestic and family violence. The persuasive interpretation of the Bible Dr. Giles gives promotes a liberating understanding of the position of women and girls and provides a charter for gender equity and the recognition of the potential of women as faith-community leaders. I very much hope that his book generates honest and open debate on domestic and family violence in our churches that results in church leaders openly opposing ideas that can result in the abuse of women."

—**Annabel Taylor**, Research Professor of Gendered Violence, Queensland Centre for Domestic and Family Violence Research

The Headship of Men and the Abuse of Women

The Headship of Men and the Abuse of Women

Are They Related In Any Way?

Kevin Giles

CASCADE *Books* · Eugene, Oregon

THE HEADSHIP OF MEN AND THE ABUSE OF WOMEN
Are They Related In Any Way?

Cascade Books
An Imprint of Wipf and Stock Publishers
199 W. 8th Ave., Suite 3
Eugene, OR 97401

www.wipfandstock.com

PAPERBACK ISBN: 978-1-7252-6138-9
HARDCOVER ISBN: 978-1-7252-6137-2
EBOOK ISBN: 978-1-7252-6139-6

Cataloguing-in-Publication data:

Names: Giles, Kevin, author.

Title: The headship of men and the abuse of women : are they related in any way? / by Kevin Giles.

Description: Eugene, OR: Cascade Books, 2020. | Includes bibliographical references and index.

Identifiers: ISBN 978-1-7252-6138-9 (paperback) | ISBN 978-1-7252-6137-2 (hardcover) | ISBN 978-1-7252-6139-6 (ebook)

Subjects: LCSH: Christian men—Family relationships. | Wife abuse—Religious aspects—Christianity

Classification: HV6626 G55 2020 (print) | HV6626 (ebook)

Manufactured in the U.S.A.   06/16/20

Content

Introduction

I SAID IN MY last book, *What the Bible Actually Teaches on Women* (Cascade, 2018) that it would be my final book. I was laying down my "pen." This did not happen. Soon after saying this, I was asked to write several articles on things close to my heart and I agreed. Then the issue of domestic abuse and violence in evangelical and Reformed churches came onto center stage at the 2018 and 2019 annual meeting of the Southern Baptist Conference in the US, and in 2018 at the annual synod of the Anglican Diocesan Synod in Sydney, Australia, two churches that are predominantly evangelical and Reformed in conviction and "complementarian" by commitment—they believe men should lead and women be "submissive" in the home and the church—and for this reason women must not be ordained as church pastors and teachers. Men should lead churches. What precipitated this debate on domestic abuse and violence in these two churches was the exposure in daily newspapers by investigative journalists of the extent of abuse in their midst, sometimes by clergy.

This public disclosure of abuse in these churches was initiated by the "MeToo" movement that began in 2017,[1] and the subsequent "ChurchToo" movement.[2] This led significant numbers of Christian women, some of them clergy wives, to say that they had been abused by their churchgoing husbands who quoted Paul's words: "the husband is the head of the wife; wives submit." Some of these women wrote to me, telling me their story. What they said really upset me. Like Jeremiah, I came to sense "something like a burning fire in my bones" (Jer 20:9) that compelled me to begin writing in their defense and against headship teaching yet again.

What greatly surprised me is how the issue of domestic abuse and violence in the homes of church members, for long years a hush-hush topic,

1. North, "7 Positive Changes"; Nicalaou and Smith, "A #MeToo Timeline."
2. Grinwold, "Silence is Not Spiritual."

1

suddenly and unexpectedly in the last two or three years has been made public and as a result forced the churches to confront this issue openly. Until very recently, virtually no Christian leader would acknowledge that domestic abuse and violence took place in Christian homes, let alone evangelical ones. The situation now is very different. A revolution has taken place.

Today,

- Virtually all church leaders acknowledge that domestic abuse is all too common in the homes of regular churchgoing families, and in clergy families.

- And, they unconditionally condemn it, calling it sinful.

What is not agreed is whether or not "headship" teaching—men are to lead in the church and the home and women are to submit—so common in some evangelical and Pentecostal churches can encourage and legitimate the abuse of women. Those who embrace headship teaching as "what the Bible clearly teaches" vehemently insist that it "neither supports nor fosters, but rather prevents and condemns, abuse."[3] They argue that there is "no causal connection between biblical teaching about a wife's submission to her husband and the scourge of domestic abuse."[4] In stark contrast, many other Christians, including many evangelical and Pentecostal ones, argue that there is "a causal connection between biblical teaching about a wife's submission to her husband and the scourge of domestic abuse."[5] It is a dangerous doctrine with malevolent consequences for many women. In this book, I put as forcefully as I can the second position. I argue headship teaching can encourage and legitimate domestic abuse and it must be abandoned if domestic abuse is to be effectively countered in our churches. I warmly commend all Christian leaders who acknowledge that domestic abuse is all too common in the homes of regular churchgoing families and who unconditionally condemn the abuse of women in the home, or any other context, as sinful. I simply disagree with those who argue that headship teaching is "what the Bible clearly teaches," that it is "good for women, good for children, and good for families,"[6] and that there is "no

3. Southern Baptist Convention, "On Abuse."

4. Anglican Diocese of Sydney, "Responding," 49.

5. This is the argument of this book, an argument that will be well-documented in what follows.

6. Moore, "After Patriarchy, What?

causal connection between biblical teaching about a wife's submission to her husband and the scourge of domestic abuse."[7]

Why I Decided to Write on Domestic Abuse and Violence

There is today a wealth of literature on domestic abuse and violence; why another book, you ask? I have a number of reasons for writing.

1. I write because as the extent and nature of domestic abuse and violence has become more fully understood and publicized in recent years, my wife Lynley, a marriage counselor, and I have wanted to play our part in combatting it in the life of the church. Knowledge and action are always dynamically related. This means that the more informed Christians become on domestic abuse and violence the more they can become part of the solution.

2. I write because I agree with Steven Tracy, an evangelical theologian, who says, "Of all the social problems confronted by the church, domestic violence is surely one of the most misunderstood and mismanaged by church leaders."[8] I want this to change.

3. I write because I have long been a sharp critic of headship teaching. I have argued over forty years that this is not the creation-ideal and it can be toxic for needy and controlling men who are present in all our churches and among the clergy. It can encourage and legitimate abuse. I am convinced that Scripture in fact makes the substantial equality of the sexes the God-given ideal. The recent public recognition that headship teaching can and often does lead to abuse and violence in churchgoing homes means the debate has taken a new turn. For the first time, those who support headship teaching are on the backfoot, taking all the punches. I write to make sure this assault on headship teaching continues and hopefully wins.

4. I write because my special field of study is what the Bible says on the man-woman relationship and on marriage. I have published widely on these related questions. My last book was titled, *What the Bible Actually Teaches on Women*. This expertise is hugely important in any discussion on domestic abuse and violence in churchgoing homes.

---

7. Anglican Diocese of Sydney, "Responding," 49.
8. Tracy, "Clergy Responses to Domestic Abuse," 9.

Virtually every male abuser with a church background quotes the Bible to justify his actions, and the church leaders who oppose abused women divorcing their husbands usually claim the Bible does not make abuse and violence a "biblical" ground for divorce or for remarriage at some later time.

5. I write because I have found that most of the best-informed articles and books on domestic abuse and violence are academic studies, not easy reading for many people. I have learnt much from them. My contribution is to summarize their most important findings in, I hope, a reader-friendly way, and relate them to our churches.

Thanks

Finally, in this introduction I thank all those who helped me in the writing of this book. First, my wife, Lynley, who critically read my work, making many valuable suggestions and comments. She is my soul-partner in life. I then sent my work to many people who I thought would be good critical readers. Some read one or two chapters, some the whole book. I thank them for giving me of their time. The readers were David Netttelbeck, Kara Hartley, Paul Collyer, Mark Thompson, Denny Burk, Wade Burlinson, Mimi Haddad, Nancy Nason-Clark, Edwina Faithful-Farmer, Andrew Newmarch, Annabel Taylor, Lesley Gray, Nicola Lock, Patti Ricotta, Steven Tracy, Kylie Maddox Pidgeon, Lynda Dunstan, and Denise Cooper-Clark. The final reader was Warren Thomas who read the proofs just before publication. I thank him for the time he gave me and praise him for extraordinary eye for detail.

I also thank my publisher, Cascade Books of Wipf and Stock Publishers, specifically my editor Chris Spinks and my copy editor Stephanie Hough. They were good to work with.

And lastly, I thank those who agreed to endorse my book—Nancy Nason-Clark, Wade Burlinson, Diphus Chemorion, Patti Ricotta, Mimi Haddad, Elaine Storkey, and Annabel Taylor.

Chapter 1

The Abuse of Women in the World and in the Church

THE PREVALENCE OF DOMESTIC abuse and violence is staggering. The figures are breath-taking and hard to believe. An unimaginable number of women's lives are blighted by this scourge. The statistics are mind-blowing. In the US, Europe, and Australia, 1 in 4 women will experience violent abuse from an intimate partner in their lifetime.[1] The incidence of abusive violence is even higher among immigrants, indigenous people, and those of color. Among indigenous women in Australia, a startling 3 in 5, or 60 percent of women, will experience violence at the hand of a partner. In the US, 43.7 percent of African American women and 37.1 percent of Hispanic/Latina women will experience violence from an intimate partner.[2] On the world scene, the United Nations estimate that 1 in 3 women (35 percent) will experience violence at the hand of an intimate partner and in some parts of the world this figure can be doubled.[3] In Australia, with a population of

1. For my statistics on the world scene, I followed Heise and Kotsadam, "Cross-National and Multilevel Correlatives of Partner Violence." On the US, I consulted Manjoo, "Violence Against Women in the United States" and "Domestic Violence Statistics." For Australia, my sources were Hill, *See What You Made Me Do;* "Change the Story"; and the Australian Institute of Health and Welfare, "Family, Domestic and Sexual Violence in Australia." Hill, *See What You Made Me Do,* 4, contests rightly the "one in six" figure quoted in some publications, for example in The Anglican Diocese of Sydney, "Responding," 27–28. *Our Watch* is an Australian group that has been established to drive nationwide change in behaviors and power imbalances that lead to violence against women and their children. They give the following figures: 1 in 3 Australian women have experienced physical violence since the age of 15; 1 in 4 Australian women have experienced physical or sexual violence by an intimate partner, and 1 in 5 Australian women have experienced sexual violence. The Australian Institute of Health and Welfare report also gives the figure, 1 in 4 women have experienced abuse from an intimate partner.

2. "Epidemiology of Domestic Violence."

3. "Facts and Figures: Ending Violence Against Women."

about 25 million, one woman a week is killed by an intimate partner, and every three hours a woman is hospitalized as a result of domestic violence. In the US, three women *per day* are killed by an intimate partner. What is so horrific is that a woman is far more likely to be abused, raped, hospitalized, or killed by someone who says they love her than by a stranger.

Many women may never be hit, never choked, never had anything thrown at them, yet they live with constant verbal abuse and put-downs, they dread the next outburst of anger directed at them, they are not free to see and do what they like, go where they wish, or spend money as they choose. They live in fear of their partner. The difference between the man who abuses his wife physically and the man who does so only in non-phys-ical ways, Lundy says, is "not as great as many believe."[4] In both, the man seeks to exercise power over his partner, to get his own way by one means or another, and the woman inevitably lives in constant fear of him.

Before going further, I need to say something about terminology and the gendered nature of "domestic abuse and violence." The first known use of the term "domestic violence," to speak of violence in a couple relation-ship, was in a report to the British Parliament in 1973. Prior to that date, the term "battered wife" and other descriptive terms were used. In recent years, the term "domestic abuse" has been preferred to make the point that most abuse in the home is not physical, such as hitting, pushing, slapping, choking, restraining, murdering.[5] Jess Hill in her 2019 comprehensive study, *See What You Made Me Do: Power, Control and Domestic Abuse*, consistently uses this term and argues it is the best term to use. All domestic abuse is certainly "violent" but not necessarily, or most commonly, physically violent. However, some social workers and counselors prefer the term "family abuse" to make the point that when abuse and violence are present in a home all the family members are impacted, the children profoundly. In this book, I speak con-sistently of "domestic abuse *and* violence" to name never-ending, controlling behavior that makes a woman live in fear of her partner.

Domestic abuse and violence is almost entirely a male sin. Women may verbally abuse their husband and hit them when they are angry, *but this is not domestic abuse and violence*. Domestic abuse is to be sharply distinguished from what is commonly called, "situational couple violence,"

---

4. Bancroft, *Why Does He Do That?* 8.

5. This is the term Hill prefers, *What You Made Me Do*. On page vii she gives her rea-sons for this. I note Anglican Diocese of Sydney, "Responding," 2, also makes "domestic abuse" the preferred term.

in which, on an occasional basis, one or both parties lash out at the other in abusive language and sometimes by hitting. Both sexes can be guilty of doing this.[6] Lundy Bancroft is crystal clear. He says, "I reserve the word *domestic abuse* for situations of control and intimidation."[7] Women do not exert power over men in the way a man can. They do not think they are entitled to be in charge, own their husband, should make all the major decisions and control the finances, or force their husband to have sex. Such behavior is *almost* exclusively gender specific. Women as a general rule cannot intimidate or instill fear in a man. No man that I have heard of secretly flees his home with his children in fear of his life. True, women can kill their partners but almost in every case this is in response to ongoing acts of violence against them, or in fear of their own murder.[8]

I am a man; I am not denigrating all men. Most men do not insist on their own way in the home at any cost and they are not abusive or violent: they are loving, caring, and respectful partners, brothers, fathers, friends and colleagues—this is what I want to be, as do most men. But around 95 percent of all violence—whether inflicted on women or men—comes by the hand of a man.[9] Men are the "heavy weight champions" when it comes to abuse and violence; they outperform women by at least nine to one.[10]

Abuse in Christian Homes

The statistics on domestic violence and abuse that I have just outlined are shocking. Even more shocking, when you are a Christian, are the rates of domestic abuse and violence in our church congregations. They are much the same as in society at large.[11] No longer can churches say things are different in the homes of our members. Churches as a general rule have not wanted to face this fact, so few studies have been done by them on this matter, but the evidence that has recently come to light means that domestic

---

6. Hill, *See What You Made Me Do*, 195–226, gives a full chapter on all this.

7. Bancroft, *Why Does He Do That?* 129.

8. Hill, *See What You Made Me Do*, 199, 223, 226.

9. "Change the Story," 20.

10. Hill, *See What You Made Me Do*, 203.

11. On domestic abuse/violence in Christian homes see Nason-Clark, *Battered Wife;* Nason-Clark and Catherine Clark Kroeger, *Refuge from Abuse;* Beck and Kroeger, *Abuse and the Bible;* Beck and Kroeger, *Healing and Hurting;* Senger, *God Hates Abuse,* and Tucker, *Black and White Bible.*

abuse and violence in churchgoing families can no longer be denied or ignored. In 1989 the Christian Reformed Church in North America conducted a random study of 1000 members; 28 percent of women said they had experienced at least one form of abuse.[12] In another American study of 1000 abused women, 67 percent indicated that they attended church regularly.[13] In Great Britain, the United Methodist Church did research on domestic violence within their churches. Reports produced on this in 2006 and 2016 indicated clearly that the number of women abused in their churches closely matched those in the wider community.[14] Similarly, the UK Anglican Archbishop's Council found in 2006, that the "incidence of domestic abuse within the church . . . is similar to the rate within the general population."[15] In Australia a 1992 study of 1704 women who were members of the Anglican or Uniting Churches, undertaken by Glenys Conrade of the University of Queensland, found 3.3 percent of women reported they had been abused in the past 12 months, 22 percent of perpetrators went to church regularly, and 14 percent were part of the church leadership.[16] In 2010 Lynne Baker reported on the basis of her PhD research that 22 percent of perpetrators of domestic abuse and violence go to church regularly— a very high percentage when only about 10 percent of Australians attend church most weeks.[17] In a 2018 survey of churchgoers in Cumbria, England, one in four respondents said that they had experienced being kicked, punched, threatened with a weapon, isolated or sexually coerced in their current relationship. And more than 40 percent of respondents said that they had experienced such abuse in a previous relationship.[18] Noticeably, the churches that would not agree to distribute the survey were "almost without exception evangelical." The researchers say, "this may suggest that evangelical churches are more reluctant than other types of church to engage with the subject of domestic abuse."[19]

---

12. Annis and Rice, "Survey of Abuse."

13. Bowker, "Religious Victims and Their Religious Leaders."

14. "Domestic Abuse—The Methodist Church," 9.

15. Church of England, "Responding Well to Domestic Abuse."

16. This reference comes from a secondary source, Yates, "Domestic Violence and Ministry Implications."

17. Baker, *Counselling Christian Women.*

18. Aune and Barnes, *In Churches Too.*

19. Aune and Barnes, *In Churches Too,* 15.

This is tragic because in conservative evangelical churches, domestic abuse and violence is far too common. It seems that they have a higher incidence of abuse in their churches and among their clergy.[20] Until recently their leaders strenuously denied this, arguing that any abuse in their homes is exceptional and that good biblical teaching tends to minimize abuse.[21] In 2017 this assertion collapsed in the wake of the Harvey Weinstein revelations. First on the hashtag "#MeToo," and then on the hashtag, "#ChurchToo" large numbers of evangelical women came forward to speak of their abuse by evangelical men, some of them clergy. Following this in December 2017, 140 well-known Christian women began an online petition, "#SilenceisNotSpiritual." Those who felt the issue of abuse of women in evangelical churches needed to be brought out into the open and things needed to change were given an opportunity to say so publicly.

These public website disclosures of abuse and violence within evangelical churches motivated investigative journalists in the US and in Australia to explore what in fact was happening in evangelical homes. What they discovered was shocking. Abuse and violence was rife and clergy were over-represented in the statistics. Two large denominational churches were caught in the spotlight: the Southern Baptist Convention and the Anglican Church in Sydney. Both are evangelical and Reformed by confession and "complementarian" by conviction. For decades, the leaders of these churches had vehemently denied that abuse and violence occurred in the homes of their church members and that their teaching on the headship of men and submission of women encouraged and legitimated domestic abuse and violence. Indeed, they claimed it countered this very thing. Let me now tell this story in more detail.

The Southern Baptist Convention

The Southern Baptist Convention (SBC) is the largest Protestant denomination in the United States. It is predominantly conservative evangelical and complementarian in theology. It began in 1845 when Baptists in the Southern states broke from the northern Baptists to form a separate pro-slavery denomination. J. Henry Thornwell who wrote the most impressive "biblical" case for slavery was a Southern Baptist.[22] Only in 1995 did the

20. Lowik and Taylor, "Evangelical Churches Believe Men Should Control Women."

21. I must have heard this said at least 1000 times.

22. On slavery in the Old South and appeals to the Bible in support by evangelicals,

SBC agree that the institution of slavery was not clearly taught in Scripture and not morally defensible. What makes the SBC distinctive among Protestants is that in its statement of faith (The Baptist Faith and Message), it sets the husband over the wife in the home and excludes women from ordination to the pastorate. In 1984 the annual SBC meeting passed a resolution prescribing that leadership in the church is male, because "the man was first in creation and the woman was first in the Edenic fall." In 1995 marriage was specifically addressed in another resolution. This said, "a wife is to submit herself to her husband. . . . She has the God-given responsibility to respect her husband and serve as his helper in managing the household and nurturing the next generation." In 2000, another resolution more emphatically excluded women from ordination as pastors.

These starkly worded resolutions, setting men over women in the home and excluding women from ordination as pastors, have not brought peace and harmony to the Southern Baptists. No issue is more contentious for them. It never goes away. Since 2003 the SBC has lost a staggering 1 million members and it is likely to lose nearly a 100,000 people each year into the foreseeable future.[23] Not all these people have left because the SBC sets men over women, but many have. The most publicized exiters, specifically on this issue, were President Jimmy Carter and his wife Rosalynn.

In the post-"MeToo" age, this simmering dispute over the status and ministry of women in the SBC came to the boil in a succession of revelations. First, in 2018, the SBC was shaken to its foundations by the Paige Patterson scandal.[24] Patterson is one of the most powerful and influential leaders in the SBC. In a transcript of a recorded address he gave in 2000 he tells a battered wife with two black eyes to stay with her husband "even if he gets a little more violent," pray for him, and at home "be as submissive in every way you can and elevate him." It was his view that abuse of one's wife is not a valid reason for divorce. When hundreds of Baptist women cried out in dismay, he at first refused to modify his words or recant them but later under huge pressure he made some ameliorating comments. This protest by women became an open letter to the trustees of Southwestern

---

see Giles, *Trinity and Subordinationism*, 215–68, and Knoll, *Civil War as a Theological Crisis*.

23. Merritt, "Southern Baptist Mid-Life Crisis."

24. There are many accounts of this sad story on the internet. I list just a few, Shellnut, "Divorce After Abuse"; Shellnut, "Paige Patterson Fired by Southwestern"; Boorstein and Pulliam, "Women Led to the Dramatic Rise and Fall"; Moss, "Paige Patterson's Views on Domestic Violence."

Baptist Theological Seminary, of which Patterson was the president. Their request was to ask him to resign, but when it came out that he had behaved improperly to women in other ways and lied to the trustees he was dismissed by them on May 30, 2018. Patterson's views are not idiosyncratic.[25] Large numbers of evangelical pastors around the world teach that abuse or violence is not a ground for divorce and a Christian wife should accept suffering in her marriage caused by her husband's words or behavior.[26] Thus the all too common advice complementarian pastors give to women who come to them telling of abuse by their husband is to tell the wife to pray for her husband, be submissive, and accept things as they are.

This initial revelation of abuse and condoning of abuse of women in the SBC opened the floodgate to further revelations. It was soon obvious that the abuse of women in their churches was endemic. In 2018 the abuse issue in the SBC became a central concern at the SBC annual meeting in Dallas. In response, the president of SBC, Pastor J. D. Greear, set up a group to draft recommendations on how to confront this huge and pressing problem, saying the SBC faced "a defining moment" that would shape the church for a generation to come.[27] At this Dallas conference, a resolution easily passed condemning domestic abuse, which stated that the Bible "neither supports nor fosters, but rather prevents and condemns, abuse."[28] The problem is that teaching the headship of men and the submission of women, a foundational doctrine of the Southern Baptists, one they claim is central to the Gospel, does seem to encourage and legitimate domestic abuse, as this book will make plain.

Pressure on the SBC to openly and honestly confront the issue of the abuse of women dramatically increased when in February 2019 *The Houston Chronicle* and *The San Antonia Express-News* published a series of articles documenting sexual abuse in the SBC. They found 380 offending clergy and at least 700 victims, and noted that the SBC had done virtually nothing about this. Stung by these articles in the press, the thousands of delegates attending the annual meeting in February 2019, in Birmingham, Alabama expected change. When the report that Pastor J. D. Greear had initiated the year before was tabled, the discussion was heated and confused. All could

---

25. See Piper, "Does a Woman Submit to Abuse?" and Moon, "Some Humans are More Equal Than Others." More will be said on this later in this book.

26. Evidence for this is given by Tracy, "Clergy Responses to Domestic Advice."

27. Reeves and Crary, "Southern Baptists Combat Sex Abuse."

28. Southern Baptist Convention, "On Abuse." I thank Denny Burk for this reference.

see the problem, but for many the issue was not the abuse of women but the implied criticism of complementarian teaching that God had given headship/leadership to men, and women are to be "submissive." One of the most startling discoveries that the authors of this SBC report found was that "sex offenders who were the most committed to church throughout their life accumulated the most victims."[29] The most significant motion passed by the 8,000 delegates was a constitutional amendment stating that member churches can be removed from SBC membership for failing to adequately address abuse issues, especially by clergy. In this debate the shocking revelation that 380 pastors had sexually abused women and children in their churches eclipsed the specific debate about the undeniable widespread domestic abuse and violence in SBC homes. The matter of domestic abuse and violence was kept off the agenda because the argument was put that this had been dealt with at the last annual meeting in 2018 in the resolution condemning domestic abuse, which I mentioned above. This of course did not, or will not, make this issue go away. The internal SBC critics publicly named the primary issues that had to be addressed, the church's "low view of women," and its teaching that men should lead in the home and the church and women are to be submissive, two related matters that they said contributes to "a culture that is friendly to abusers."[30]

What this SBC annual meeting made plain was that the abuse of women as individuals could not be separated from its headship teaching that implied the secondary status of women in the church and the home. "The woman problem" in Southern Baptists Churches is just one of the many huge challenges this denomination faces, possibly its most pressing and important one, and one that the church is unable to address because they have made the hierarchical ordering of the sexes a matter of faith. They have claimed this is what a true Christian should believe. This is costing the church dearly.

The Anglican Diocese of Sydney and Domestic Abuse

The Anglican Diocese of Sydney is one of the largest and wealthiest Anglican Dioceses in the world. Like the Southern Baptists, it is predominantly evangelical by confession and complementarian by conviction. Its one seminary, Moore Theological College, is where I did my initial studies.

29. Carter, "FAQs."
30. Gjelten, "Southern Baptists to Confront Sexual Abuse."

Sydney Anglican theologians and bishops have long argued that their faithful exposition of Paul's teaching on "male headship" and female "submission" could in no way encourage domestic abuse and violence in their homes; indeed, it is a counter force. Mark Thompson, the principal of Moore Theological College, Sydney is on record as saying publicly, "Biblical headship and submission is not the cause [of domestic abuse], *in fact it is quite the opposite.*"[31] In 2018 this response to domestic abuse and violence in their churches and homes collapsed when two investigative journalists, Julia Baird and Hayley Gleeson, wrote a number of articles on domestic abuse in the Anglican Church in Sydney.[32] They found wife abuse was all too common in regularly attending families and in clergy families. They also reported that clergy were often dismissive of complaints by women of their husband's behavior, and they were seldom helpful to the women who came to them for help and guidance in a domestic crisis. Significantly, the wives they interviewed who had been abused spoke of how their abusing husband had consistently appealed to headship teaching and to Paul's exhortations to wives to be submissive. This was a consistent and repeated comment.

These articles empowered first one clergy wife of a Moore College trained clergyman to bravely come forward and publicly say that her husband had repeatedly abused her and sometimes had been violent to her. As a result, she had left the marriage in fear of her life. Then other clergy wives stepped forward and said the same, and soon after this women married to lay leaders stood up to express the same concerns.[33] The predominant response from Sydney church leaders was to attack these two courageous female journalists. They were demonized as critics of the Sydney Anglican Church and of the Christian faith.

These newspaper articles, like the ones in the US, meant that no longer could it be denied that domestic abuse and violence were endemic in the Sydney Diocese. It was now public knowledge. This issue could not be ignored, or the reality in the church denied any longer. In 2017 the Diocese set up a task force to do a thorough study on this matter and to formulate future diocesan policy and practice. In 2018 at the annual synod the report

31. Anglican Diocese of Sydney, "Responding," 51. Italics added.

32. Baird and Gleeson, "Submit to your Husbands" and "Domestic Violence in the Church."

33. "Abused Clergy Wife's Message to the Church." See also an earlier article by a battered wife of a lay preacher; Young, "Abuse Inside Christian Marriages"; Baird and Gleeson, "Abuse Inside Christian Marriages."

of 62 pages was unanimously accepted and made diocesan policy. In this document, domestic abuse is condemned and called "sinful." It acknowledges that domestic abuse takes place in the homes of regular churchgoers and that clergy are among the offenders. There are three long sections on how to deal with offending clergy and how to support their wives. Twenty-three times the "headship" of men and the "submission" of women is affirmed explicitly. Repeatedly, this document asserts in various wording that there is no "causal connection between the biblical teaching about a wife's submission to her husband and the scourge of domestic abuse."[34] In an addendum at the end of this book I summarize this document in more detail and critically evaluate it.

The Debate that Followed

Following the tabling and acceptance of this document, a large percentage of synod members wanted a motion put, stating publicly that abuse and violence in a marriage were a valid reason for divorce. The power brokers in the diocese were opposed to this because for them the Bible only gave two grounds for divorce, adultery (Matt 19:9), and desertion (1 Cor 7:15). They thus carefully worded the motion that went before the chair of synod.[35] The motion asked the archbishop or regional bishops to approve "the *remarriage* of a divorced person, where that person has been abused physically or emotionally by their former spouse."[36] The motion was worded in this way because the opponents did not want to be seen as opposing an abused woman leaving her marriage, possibly in fear of her life. Opposing *remarriage* was less of a problem. This made for a very confusing debate.[37] In the

34. Anglican Diocese of Sydney, "Responding," 49.

35. Jensen, *Sydney Anglicanism*, has a very interesting chapter, 160–72, on how politics is played in the Anglican Diocese of Sydney. It is very much a hard ball game.

36. Italics added. The exact wording of this motion is as follows, "Synod, noting that it is the prerogative of the Archbishop or a Regional Bishop, in accordance with the laws of this Church, whether or not to approve the remarriage of a divorced person, requests the Archbishop and Regional Bishops to consider approving the remarriage of a divorced person, where that person has been abused physically or emotionally by their former spouse." I thank Kara Hartley for this.

37. Gleeson and Baird, "No Brainer." I was not present but a woman at this synod sent me her typed-up account of who spoke and what they said, and I sent a copy of this chapter to Archbishop Glen Davies, Mark Thompson, Kara Hartley, and one other person who did not want to be named to verify. Archbishop Davies did not reply, Mark Thompson replied asking me to make a few cosmetic word changes which I did. Kara

minds of most of those present in synod if someone is validly divorced, then they can remarry. Divorce annuls marriage vows. Once the debate began the real issue in contention soon became apparent. Those opposed were convinced that domestic abuse and violence were not "biblical" grounds for divorce. Dr. Mark Thompson, the principal of Moore College, led the opposition. He said, "We must be very careful that in our right and proper concern for the victims of domestic abuse, we do not redraw our doctrine of marriage."[38] Bishop Peter Lin, also speaking in opposition, was even more explicit. He said as awful as abuse and violence in a marriage might be, the Bible did not allow this to be a valid reason for divorce. In opposing the motion, several speakers appealed to 1 Pet 3:1–6, where they believed the Bible asked married Christian women to accept abuse and violence at the hand of their husband. Others quoted Mal 2:16, following the RSV and NRSV translation, "I hate divorce says the Lord."

All those in favor of the motion, like those in opposition, saw the issue as whether or not abuse and violence in a marriage is a valid reason to leave one's husband and divorce him, and they were convinced it is. They won the day. As the debate drew to a close, Robert Tong, a strong opponent of the motion, moved that it be a secret ballot. This did not help him or his friends. The motion was carried 325 to 161. What is remarkable is that 161 voters were convinced that a Christian woman should not divorce her husband no matter how abusive and violent he might be, even if she was in fear of her life and that of her children! Their "biblical" view of marriage could not allow it. Upholding their doctrine of marriage was more important than protecting women.

Archbishop Glen Davies, himself a conservative evangelical and complementarian, and who was chairing the synod, said that for him personally this is one of the "most contentious and difficult issues that I have had to deal with."[39] Why this matter was for him, and the 161 opponents of the motion, so difficult is clear. It was expressed many times by speakers against the motion. Scripture gives no explicit basis for a woman to divorce her husband for abuse or violence.

Hartley also asked for a few corrections which I made. She also gave me added information which I included.

38. I thank Mark Thompson for sending me a copy of his speech at the synod. I quote from this.

39. Quote given by Baird, "After Years of Debate."

This appeal to the Bible in opposition to allowing that abuse and violence in a marriage is a valid reason for divorce is abysmal. It is "proof-texting" at its worst. To believe that "my interpretation" of one or two texts can be the basis for what I would call "Christian theology" or ethical decision making is naïve and mistaken.[40] Theology needs to be predicated on what is foundational in Scripture on any issue, and surely basic to Scripture is the demand that a man love his wife like Christ loved the church; he should act towards her as he would like her to act towards him, and violence is never pleasing to God. Later, in chapter 4, I will carefully consider what 1 Pet 3:1–6 and Mal 2:16 are most likely saying, but surely common sense should tell us that for a man to habitually abuse his wife and at times be violent to her annuls the marriage vows as much as adultery. For me, the God revealed in Jesus Christ would not expect a woman in fear of her life and possibly the life of her children to stay in her marriage at any cost. I do not need a text to convince me of this. If anyone thinks otherwise, I can only conclude there is something unbalanced in their theology. They are like the Pharisees of old who could justify their behavior by appeal to a text (Matt 5:21–47; 15:1–20; 19:1–7; 22:23–33; 23:1–36; etc.) and yet Jesus judged them to be in error, calling them "hypocrites" (Matt 7:5; Luke 6:42; 13:15; etc.). In chapter 4, where I deal with what the Bible says on marriage and divorce, I will discuss how 1 Peter 2–3 should be rightly interpreted, arguing that Peter does not make unjust suffering for slaves or wives a virtue.

The next matter on the 2018 Synod agenda was far more positive and gained full support. Synod was agreed that an apology was due to the numerous women who had been abused in the diocese and ignored or criticized by the clergy they looked to for support, and something needed to be done to support the many abused clergy wives who had been forced to leave their marriage and their church-supplied home. This led to a motion being put and passed, apologizing to all the abused women in the diocese, and for the way they had been treated.[41] In addition, the Synod passed a motion to set up a "Ministry Spouse Support Fund," which would allow clergy wives who had been abused by their ordained husband and had left

40. I have discussed the nature of evangelical theology in several of my publications. See my most recent work on this matter, Giles, *Rise and Fall of the Complementarian Doctrine.*

41. Gleeson and Baird, "Anglican Diocese of Sydney Makes an Apology"; Gleeson, "Church Confesses to Domestic Violence in its Ranks"; "Australian Churches Risk Becoming a Haven for Abusers."

the marriage and their home to access an initial sum of $10,000, followed by a one-off grant of $50,000.

This did not make the matter of domestic abuse go away. It still occurs far too often in the diocese and the abuse of women issue continues to divide Sydney Anglicans, some blaming the incessant headship teaching in their churches and others claiming this teaching in no way encourages men to be abusive. Following Mark Thompson, they argue, it does "quite the opposite"; it counters domestic abuse. The issue of the abuse of women in church homes is of course just one specific instance of what is often called in Sydney "the woman problem" that bedevils the life of the diocese. It is like a festering sore that will not heal. In the modern world, insisting that men lead and women be submissive in the home, and excluding women from church leadership, makes no sense to most people and it is offensive. It implies that women are second-class members of the church. This teaching hurts the church deeply and it is eroding membership. It is a huge hinderance to evangelism in Sydney.

Listening to the Voice of Abused Christian Women

In a subsequent chapter I will refer to what we learn about domestic abuse and violence in the scholarly literature but at this point I want to encourage my readers to search out accounts of domestic abuse, especially by Christian men, including some pastors. I make this plea because far too many conservative evangelical leaders are hugely resistant to acknowledging that domestic abuse and violence is predominantly a male sin; hugely resistant to accepting that it is all too common in families that regularly attend church and in minister's homes; and hugely resistant to the argument that headship/submission teaching can encourage and legitimate domestic violence in needy and controlling men. Today there are innumerable true-life accounts in books, articles, and especially online by Christian women on how they have been abused by their Christian husband, some of them evangelical pastors.

For your information, I mention two published true-life accounts that I found very powerful and informative. First, Ruth Tucker's *Black and White Bible, Black and Blue Wife—My Story of Finding Hope After Domestic Abuse*. Ruth holds a PhD from Northern Illinois University, and was a professor of theology at Trinity Evangelical School and Calvin Theological Seminary, prestigious evangelical institutions, before her retirement.

She has authored 17 books. In this book she recounts her harrowing story of abuse at the hands of her husband, an evangelical pastor of Reformed convictions, well-educated, articulate, and charming in public. In telling of her personal experience of domestic abuse, she weaves together stories of other abused women married to evangelical Christians. For nineteen years she endured all manner of abuse: verbal, emotional, sexual, spiritual, and physical. The spiritual abuse involved his constant appeal to the Bible. He insisted that the Bible clearly taught that he was the head of the home and she should obey him. She says,

> During his violent rages, my ex-husband often hurled biblical texts at me, as though the principal tenet of Scripture was, "Wives, submit to your husbands." He'd spit the words out repeatedly, beating me over the head, at least figuratively, with his black-and-white Bible. His hitting and punching and slamming me, however, were anything but figurative. Nor were his terror-loaded threats. I felt trapped and feared for my life, while outwardly disguising bruises with long sleeves and clever excuses, pretending ours was a happy marriage.[42]

Second, I mention Robin Mullins Senger's book, *God Hates Abuse: Abuse and the Doctrine of Headship and Submission*.[43] She says her book "grew out of my journey of recovery and healing from a dangerous and abusive marriage."[44] Robin was married for more than ten years to an abusive and violent husband, an evangelical who knew the Bible well, who insisted that he was "the head of the home" and thus should be obeyed. Then one day it all became too much and she fled, going into hiding with her three children in fear of her life and theirs. She vividly tells of what went on in her marriage with the intent of helping other Christian wives in similar abusive and violent relationships. The biographical nature of her story, like that of Ruth Tucker's, makes it compelling reading.

The Questions Before Us

What has been said in this chapter forcefully throws up three closely related questions. Why do some men abuse their wives? Why do some

---

42. Tucker, *Black and White Bible*, 14.

43. Senger, *God Hates Abuse*, first published 2016, second edition updated and expanded, 2019.

44. Senger, *God Hates Abuse*, 1.

Christian men abuse their wives? And, why do conservative evangelical men more than other men abuse their wives? In what follows I will seek to answer these questions. The fact that Christian men are percentage-wise just as likely—or even possibly more likely—to abuse their wives is counterintuitive. You would think that biblical teaching on love of neighbor, love of wife, forgiveness, humility, and servant leadership would counter any thought that a Christian husband would forcefully impose his will on his wife and abuse her.

The fact that some abusers are pastors, most of evangelical and Reformed conviction, is the most difficult thing to comprehend. Does not Paul say, "Husbands love your wives, just as Christ loved the church and gave himself up for her"? And does not Paul expect church leaders to be "above reproach," "not a drunkard, not violent, but gentle, not quarrelsome," and "self-controlled" (1 Tim 3:1–3; Titus 1:7–8)? We can only ask, are abusing Christian husbands so transfixed by their favorite text, Eph 5:22, "Wives be subject to your husbands . . . for the husband is the head of the wife," that they cannot see what else Scripture says on the husband-wife relationship, and specifically on the need for a Christian man to love his wife like Christ loved the church and gave his life for her?

Chapter 2

Understanding Domestic Abuse and Violence

BEFORE ANY INFORMED AND helpful discussion on domestic abuse and violence can take place, we must clearly understand what this involves. We are not talking about robust arguments and violent acts done in anger that may occur between a couple periodically—what is commonly called "situational couple violence." Domestic abuse refers to *the ongoing assertion of power*, almost always by the man over his wife or intimate partner, that has as its intent the complete control of the woman.[1] The best *description* of what domestic abuse and violence involves I found in Lundy Bancroft's superb book, *Why Does He Do That? Inside the Head of Angry and Controlling Men.*[2] If you want to understand domestic violence and abuse, this book is a must read. I would love to see Bancroft's book made compulsory reading for every theological student and one on the bookshelf of every pastor.

In the light of working with more than 2000 "angry and abusive men," Bancroft concludes that they fall into a spectrum of behaviors that distinguish them from most men. I draw heavily on his work but add to it in the light of the comments made by readers of this chapter, some of them women who have been abused, and from my wider reading. An abusive man typically exhibits several, and sometimes most, of the following characteristics:

1. *He is controlling.* An abusive man wants to control every aspect of his intimate partner's life: what she thinks, who she sees, how she dresses, how she does her hair, how she disciplines the children, when she gets home, what she reads and watches on TV, how she spends money, and much more. He must have the final say. What he does, he insists, he does for her good. He knows what is best for "them."

---

1. Domestic abuse of course always bears on the children in the family in many ways.
2. Bancroft, *Why Does He Do That?*

2. *He feels entitled.* It is his belief that as the man in the home he should make all the major decisions because he is the natural leader. He believes that his preeminence in the relationship gives him "exclusive rights and privileges."[3] This sense of entitlement, more than anything else, Bancroft says, characterizes the abusive man.

3. *He believes men and women are inherently different.* Men are "strong, independent, unemotional, logical and confident," women are "expressive, nurturant, weak and dependent."[4]

4. *He is possessive.* He thinks he owns his partner. She is his, and his alone. He is pathologically jealous, hating to see her talking or working closely with another man, or spending time with friends or members of her family. He wants her all for himself. His goal is to isolate her so she is dependent and focused on him alone.

5. *He is frequently angry/enraged.* Because the abuser has unfair and unrealistic expectations of his partner, he often gets angry because she hasn't done what he told her or has done something of which he does not approve. He uses his anger to get her to comply with his wishes and demands.

6. *He twists things into the opposite.* "The abusers highly entitled perceptual system causes him to mentally reverse aggression and self-defense."[5] Nothing provokes him more than his female partner defending herself or arguing with him. He says, "I am angry because you made me angry." When she does not immediately do what he demands, he sees it as a threat to his right to be in charge and to determine everything. Jess Hill, in her lengthy study of domestic abuse, entitles her book, "*See what you made me do.*" The abusive man's insistence on interpreting everything from his own perspective characterizes his way of thinking. Many abused women say, "He twists my mind." This is often called "gaslighting."[6]

---

3. Bancroft, *Why Does He Do That?*, 54

4. Hill, *See What You Made Me Do*, 135, 105, 115–16. "Change the Story," 25.

5. Bancroft, *Why Does He Do That?*, 61.

6. This term is used to refer to a form of psychological manipulation in which a person seeks to sow seeds of doubt in the mind of another person, making them question their own memory, perception, and sanity. The term originated from the 1938 Patrick Hamilton play *Gaslight* and its 1940 and 1944 film adaptations, in which the gas-fueled lights in a character's home are dimmed when he turns the attic lights brighter while he searches the attic at night. He convinces his wife that she is imagining the change. See

7. *He is manipulative.* In one situation he uses his anger to get his own way, in another situation he expresses love and affection for his partner to get his own way.

8. *He strives to have a good public image.* Abusers characteristically are warm and charming in public social settings and quite the opposite in the home. They are Dr. Jekyll and Mr. Hyde. People see them as friendly, charming, humorous, and competent. Thus, if people hear that a wife or intimate partner has accused a man of being abusive, they simply cannot believe it. They think she must have caused the problem. I once worked with a fellow minister who preached like the angel Gabriel, was humorous and charming at morning tea, and loved by all the women in the congregation, but at home with his wife he was like a bear with a sore head. He was abusive in many ways. She feared displeasing him.

9. *He justifies his behavior.* Abusing men can justify everything they do and cannot admit to any failure on their part. The abuser may say, "It was just a push when she pressed my buttons," or "She made me do it," or "If she had not said or done that, I would not have got angry."

10. *He uses sex to exert his power and to further his own goals.* Many women in an abusive relationship come to recognize that sex for them is not a wonderful, free-giving of oneself in love. Her partner demands sex when and wherever he wants it, insisting that it is his right to have sex as often as he likes. A significant number of abusive men are promiscuous (it is their right to do as they like) and addicted to pornography. Pornography is a problem because first of all it depersonalizes women, depicting them predominantly in sexual terms. It assumes that human sex is purely physical—cut off from the whole person, without any hint of love or commitment. Then there is the problem that most of it today is hardcore porn—known as "gonzo," which degrades women, and is all too commonly physically violent.[7]

The behavior of abusers and their tactics are not the same in every home, but there is a surprising constancy. Hill says, "It's as if they've studied some kind of domestic abuse handbook."[8]

---

also Hill, *See What You Made Me Do,* 30.

7. Hill, *See What You Made Me Do,* 146–48.

8. Hill, *See What You Made Me Do,* 13.

Types of Abuse

Abuse may involve some or all of the following.

- *Verbal abuse*: including devaluing comments, continual putdowns, constant criticism, angry outbursts almost invariably involving swearing, sarcasm, ridicule.

- *Emotional/psychological abuse:* blaming the woman for all the problems in the relationship; turning around everything she says; "gaslighting"; constantly comparing her with other women; magnifying every mistake she makes and constantly reminding her of this; giving her the silent treatment; sleeping in another room; etc.

- *Social abuse:* restricting or controlling contact with friends or family; forbidding her to go out to social gatherings; constant and cutting criticism of her family and friends; and tracking her movements on "spyware." His goal is to isolate her.

- *Financial/economic abuse*: having control of all monies; granting no access to bank accounts; doling out money for household accounts reluctantly; criticizing her spending; etc.

- *Spiritual abuse*: quoting the Bible to justify his behavior; insisting that he is more spiritual or more obedient as a Christian; belittling her faith; denigrating her pastor and church; etc.

- *Sexual abuse*: being forced or coerced into unwanted sex; doing things she finds objectionable; forcing her to watch pornography; etc.

- *Physical abuse*: hitting, punching, pushing, choking, throwing things, restraining, murdering.

Domestic abuse is always ultimately about power in one way or another; the man feels he must be in control.[9] His male identity as a leader must be asserted. Jess Hill says, "The unifying ingredient among abusers is a radioactive sense of entitlement"—"I should be in charge."[10] But power can be exercised in different ways. How this power is experienced is not the same for all women in abusive and violent relationships. Domestic abuse occurs on a spectrum of power and control. Some abusers are dictators, seeking to control every part of their partner's life. They tend to act

---

9. Hill, *See What You Made Me Do*, 22, 24.
10. Hill, *See What You Made Me Do*, 150.

like drill sergeants. They seek to get their own way all the time at any cost. Women live in fear of their anger. At the other end stand abusers who are less dominating and threatening. They do not completely subordinate their partners but they nevertheless want to be in control and their partners certainly fear crossing them.[11] Bancroft gives a more nuanced and descriptive account of abusers, listing ten variants.[12]

It is also important to know that "life with an abuser can be a dizzy wave of exciting good times and at the same time, painful periods of verbal, physical and sexual assault."[13] No abuser is constantly abusive; often he can be loving, generous, and kind.

Now let me make the point again: domestic abuse and violence is almost entirely a male sin. Most couples have arguments, and the man or the woman may raise their voice and even hit their partner but this is not domestic abuse. It is only domestic abuse when the anger is aimed at controlling the other person, in a way that provokes fear. Annette Gillespie is the head of Victoria's Safe Steps Family Violence Response Centre. She says,

> I think there's a tremendous amount of confusion in the community about the difference between family violence[14] and relationship conflict. People really struggle to understand that for family violence to be present, there are two key attributes to it. One of them is that one party is in fear of the other. The other is that the abuser uses a planned, systematic approach to remove a person's confidence, support networks and independence in order to highlight their own power and control within the relationship.
>
> Most people have arguments with the person they love. It's normal to feel jealous, say things you regret, even scream the house down. It only becomes domestic violence when this is bent towards controlling the other person, in a way that provokes fear. There is another thing people are confused about. When I do presentations on domestic violence, I now start by saying, "Let's get this question out of the way," because someone is sitting there waiting to say it. Do women abuse as much as men? No. The idea that domestic violence is "gender equal," and that women's violence against men is a silent "epidemic," is nonsense.

11. Hill, See *What You Made Me Do*, 20.

12. Bancroft, *Why Does He Do That?*, 76–104.

13. Bancroft, *Why Does He Do That?*, 147.

14. I note she uses the term "family violence," where I prefer the term "domestic abuse."

When men's groups claim that one in three victims of family violence is male, they promote a dangerous fiction.[15]

What Causes Some Men to Abuse the Woman Whom They Say They Love?

Historically, men's abuse of and violence towards women have been explained primarily in individualistic terms. Such explanations find the cause in the psychology, mental health, or life experiences of perpetrators. While these personal factors may certainly play a part and should not be ignored, they are inadequate on their own. The scholarly consensus today is that behind all domestic abuse and violence lies a belief in male privilege and entitlement, and conversely, a low estimation of women, that usually reflects the values and ideas of the community in which people find themselves. In their comprehensive study of domestic violence, "Change the Story," *Our Watch* puts it this way,

> Although there is no single cause of violence against women and their children, the latest international evidence shows that there are certain factors that consistently predict—or drive—higher levels of violence against women. These include beliefs and behaviors reflecting disrespect for women, low support for gender equality and an adherence to or rigid or stereotyped gender roles, relations and identities.[16]

These beliefs, they add, reflect taken-for-granted social and cultural norms of a given community, that are invariably reflected in the practices and behavior of these communities and their institutions.

This is what we may call the *macro-level* explanation of domestic abuse and violence, but this alone does not explain why *some* men in any community are violent (or more violent) towards their partner than others. What we must accept is that there are *macro-level* drivers and *micro-level* drivers of domestic abuse and violence; societal factors and individual factors, play their part and are almost always in interaction in any one abuser.[17] At the macro and societal level, the focus falls on

---

15. Quoted by, Hill, "Costs and Causes of Domestic Violence."

16. "Change the Story," Foreword, 1.

17. Carlson, "Causes and Maintenance of Domestic Abuse"; Heise and Kotsadam, "Cross-National and Multilevel Correlates of Partner Abuse," 332–40; "Change the Story," 21–23.

how social norms, cultural values, and religious belief systems impact behavior. At the micro and individual level, the focus falls on what each person brings to the couple relationship; their family history; their sense of self-worth; their identity as a man or a woman; how they have learned to get their own way; their mental health; etc.

This multi-faceted and interactive explanation of domestic abuse and violence is called "the ecological" explanation. In biology, this term refers to the presupposition that organisms are in relation to other organisms and in relation to their physical surroundings. When used metaphorically of the couple relationship, the presupposition is that any two people in a couple relationship are set in a social world where certain norms and behavior are assumed, and each person in that relationship tends to act in characteristic ways learnt in their lifetime and that always these two things are in interaction.

Before going further, I need to say something on the word "cause." Nothing *causes*, in the sense of "makes," someone abusive. Men living in starkly patriarchal cultures, men with wounded psyches, men who get angry quickly, men who drink too much, men whose dad abused their mother, etc., are not *necessarily* abusive of the women they live with. Some are not. Thus, in this usage, the word "cause" carries the weaker sense of *what may produce abuse* in an intimate relationship. To overcome the problems with this word, some researchers speak rather of "drivers"—what moves someone to go in a certain direction.

The Macro-level Explanation

The macro-level explanation of domestic abuse and violence must be discussed first because it is of first importance. In the contemporary scholarly literature, the consensus is that behind all domestic abuse and violence lies the belief that men should be in charge and make all the important decisions and women should be submissive.

Heise and Kotsadam in their 2015 *Lancet* article based on 66 surveys, in 44 countries and involving 481 subjects found that "especially predictive . . . of partner violence are norms related to male authority."[18] And, "The

---

18. Heise and Kotsadam, "Cross-National and Multilevel Correlates of Partner Abuse," 347.

main drivers of partner violence are gender related norms and hierarchies that shape relationships between men and women."[19]

In other words, where communities believe that men are privileged and should be in charge and women submissive, women in much higher percentages are abused.

Liz Wall in her important article, "Gender Equality and Violence Against Women," makes the same point:

> A lack of gender equality is consistently cited as an underlying determinant of violence against women. The United Nations General Assembly, in its 1993 Declaration on the Elimination of Violence Against Women, noted that this violence is a manifestation of historically unequal power relations between men and women. Gender inequality as a cause of violence against women also underpins approaches to prevention by organizations such as the World Health Organization and, in Australia, VicHealth, as well as much of the research on the topic.
>
> Research has constantly found that men who hold traditional hierarchical views about gender roles and relationships are more likely to perpetuate violence against women.[20]

Jess Hill agrees:

> It is indisputable that traditional notions of masculinity—particularly male entitlement—are at the core of men's violence against women.[21]

And surprisingly, Professor Steven Tracy (who calls himself a "soft complementarian"), is of the same mind:

> Models of patriarchy which give husbands the greatest levels of power and authority are most likely to stimulate domestic violence.[22]

> There is abundant data showing that conceptions of gender in which males are viewed as superior to females and in which males are attributed greater power to control females are predictors of increased levels of domestic violence.[23]

19. Heise and Kotsadam, "Cross-National and Multilevel Correlates of Partner Violence," 336. This is put as a thesis to be tested. It is found correct by the research.

20. Wall, "Gender Equality and Violence Against Women," 2.

21. Hill, *See What You Made Me Do*, 109.

22. Tracy, "Patriarchy and Domestic Violence," 42.

23. Tracy, "Asking Christians to do Better."

This macro-level explanation of domestic abuse and violence is often called the "patriarchal" or "feminist" explanation, usually pejoratively by conservative Christians. It is best called the scientific and most compelling explanation. The term "patriarchy" literally means "the rule of the father," or more broadly, the rule of the oldest man in an extended family. Patriarchy is predicated on male entitlement. It speaks of the belief that men should be in charge; men are born to lead; women to follow. In other words, men and women are inherently different. Study after study has found that men who have internalized these beliefs and own them are more prone to be abusers.[24]

The patriarchal premise that men should lead, women be submissive, is as old as humankind and it still prevails in many parts of the world. It is reflected in all the holy writings of all the great religions of the world, including Christianity. This is to be expected because all these writings were written by those who assumed patriarchy. It was for them taken-for-granted. This means religion can powerfully reinforce patriarchal beliefs and specifically it can be used to justify men asserting their authority and control over women. For religion to become a liberating force in opposition to domestic abuse and violence, the leaders of each religion need to accept that what they find in their scriptures seeming to endorse male privilege is only a reflection of a past age, never the ideal.

In answer to the argument that patriarchal beliefs are the foundational "cause" of domestic abuse and violence, critics point out that in modern Western societies, with their ever-growing gender equality, domestic abuse and violence remain pervasive, possibly on the increase. The Nordic countries are often cited. In these countries gender equality is pursued rigorously—they are sometimes called "gender equal utopias"—yet domestic abuse and violence hover around 30 percent—higher than the European average of 22 percent, the United States average of 24 percent, and the Australian average of 25 percent.[25] There is not a great difference in these numbers, and certainly the statistics are approximations, but what is clear is that an increase in gender equality appears to push up abuse statistics.

---

24. Hill, *See What You Made Me Do,* 103 and esp. Wall, "Gender Equality and Violence Against Women."

25. Hill, *See What You Made Me Do,* 128.

Complementarians incessantly note this fact, arguing that it proves that gender inequality is not the cause of domestic abuse and violence.[26] This is not a compelling argument. We should expect

- violence against women to increase when men feel their power and control is slipping away.

- the empowerment of women to make men in patriarchal cultures, and needy and controlling men in Western egalitarian cultures, more anxious about their status.

- some men to feel their masculinity is being threatened when women act independently and assertively.[27]

- a male backlash against the emancipation of women.

In migrant communities that have come from patriarchal cultures to Australia, and to other Western countries, we see examples of what I have just argued. The new freedoms that women find in their new culture often lead to their abuse as their husbands sense their power over them is under threat.

Micro-level Explanations

Many books and articles coming from the First World on domestic abuse and violence focus mainly on individual causation. Heise and Kotsadam see this as a consequence of the authors living in a profoundly egalitarian and individualistic culture where patriarchy is not the social norm.[28] When all attention is given to what drives or causes *individual men* to be abusive of their partner, the psyche of the man becomes the main focus. As abusive men differ greatly from each other, many different and often competing explanations are given.

One of the most common explanations at an individual level is that something is wrong with the minds of male abusers to make them behave

26. In an addendum at the end of this book, "Headship Teaching Does Not Encourage or Legitimate Domestic Abuse," I list and answer the various arguments complementarians use to deflect any suggestion that headship teaching could encourage churchgoing men to be abusive or violent. In this, I again point out why the emancipation of women may at first increase abuse.

27. Hill, *See What You Made Me Do,* 8, calls this a "backlash" against women's empowerment.

28. So Heise and Kosalam, "Cross-National and Multilevel Correlates of Partner Abuse," 335.

in this controlling way. The "wiring" in their brains is different to most men. The problem is that most abusers seem very normal. They think rationally, can explain their actions, hold down jobs, and relate well in social settings. Jess Hill says,

> It would be easier for us to believe that domestic abusers are recognizably different from normal men. But we cannot avoid the uncomfortable truth that violent and sadistic behavior can come from otherwise "normal" minds.[29]

This of course is not to deny that *some* abusive men are driven by psychopathological forces. Perpetrators of domestic abuse consistently show a higher than average incidence of common psychological disorders.[30]

Another popular micro-level explanation is that abusive men have a sense of "compromised masculinity."[31] They feel shame that they are powerless as men so they seek to exert power over their intimate partner. Shame speaks of feeling that one is not worthy, one is less than one ought to be, one has been humiliated. Male shame, Hill says, is "built around one unbreakable rule; do not be weak. To be a man is to be strong, powerful and in control."[32] In their relationship with their partner, abusive men who do not feel powerful exert power over their partner to assuage their sense of powerlessness. They do it in the home because in the home they can do it. The minute they feel their power is being challenged they come out fighting. To put it succinctly, male abusers are *needy men*.

Another micro explanation is that abusing men cannot control their anger. Lundy Bancroft in his superb book, *Why Does He Do That?* very helpfully discusses this suggestion. He cogently argues that abusing men are *not* exceptionally angry men, but rather men who have learned that anger enables them to get their own way. It is a means to an end. He says we all get angry at times but in most cases, this does not lead to abusive behavior.[33]

Alcohol is also given as the cause of much domestic abuse, and certainly it is a factor in many instances. Nancy Nason-Clark says one study

---

29. Hill, *See What You Made Me Do*, 103–4. See also Bancroft, *Why Does He Do That?*, 38–39.

30. Tracy, "Patriarchy and Domestic Abuse," 13–14 outlines the evidence for this. See also Hill, *See What You Made Me Do*, 101 and Senger, *God Hates Divorce*, 229–32.

31. *Hill, See What You Made Me Do*, 112, and all of chapter 4, 111–33. See also Dutton with Galant, *Batterer*.

32. Hill, *See What You Made Me Do*, 115.

33. Bancroft, *Why Does He Do That?*, 37–38.

found that abuse in 40 percent of cases followed the consumption of alcohol, and that women who lived with men who drank heavily were at far greater risk of assault than women who lived with men who did not drink.[34] Alcohol is a disinhibitor, allowing people to behave in ways they would not when they are sober. In other words, when a man has drunk too much his controlling and abusive anger can be given free reign. However, like anger, alcohol does not *cause* abusive behavior.[35] Some men when they drink too much become genial teddy bears.

Finally, I mention the impact of witnessed abuse and violence in the home on children. For daughters, this is an awful experience that never leaves them and often crushes their sense of self-worth as a woman, and all too often leads them to marry an abusive man. Sons, on their part, who see their father abusing their mother and being violent are far more likely to later abuse their wife. Nason-Clark says it is estimated that between 50 and 75 percent of wife abusers saw abuse and violence in their original home.[36] Lundy Bancroft says, "Boys who grow up in homes where their mother is battered are more likely than other boys to grow up to abuse their own wives and girlfriends."[37] This may be called the *intergenerational transmission* of domestic abuse and violence.

Now to sum up: what is so helpful with the ecological model of explanation is that we do not have to choose between macro and micro explanations, or between any one micro explanation and another to explain the abusive behavior of an individual man. We can concede that many things can drive a man to be abusive of and violent towards the woman he says he loves. What we do know for certain, nevertheless, is that all abusive men have a sense of entitlement; they believe because they are a man they should be in control; they should make all the important decisions; and their wife should be submissive. The micro or individual drivers of domestic abuse and violence simply personalize how this primary belief is expressed.

34. Nason-Clark, *Battered Wife*, 6.

35. See Bancroft, *Why Does He Do That?*, 201–3.

36. Nason-Clark, *Battered Wife*, 9.

37. Bancroft, *When Dad Hurts Mum*, 313. Steven Tracy in his article, "Clergy Responses to Domestic Abuse," 13, similarly says this is "the most common factor among men who abuse their wives."

What Causes Some Christian Men to Abuse the Woman Whom They Say They Love?

What I have just outlined prepares us well to answer this question, but before I say anything on this matter I need to tell my readers who are not familiar with intramural church debates over what the Bible says about women and marriage, that evangelical Christians are deeply and profoundly divided into two camps on what in fact the Bible teaches on the man-woman relationship. On one side stand those who call themselves "complementarians," and the other side those who call themselves, "evangelical egalitarians." I first outline the complementarian position in *plain English*. Complementarians teach that in creation before the fall, God set the man over the woman and thus the hierarchical ordering of the sexes is God-given, good, and can never change. Men and women are not equal in any substantive sense; men are to rule over women; women are to be submissive. In the 2018 Anglican Diocese of Sydney document, "Responding to Domestic Abuse," written within a "complementarian framework," we are told twenty-three times that the complementarian position takes as its basic presupposition "the headship" of men and "the submission" of women.[38] The title of David Pawson's book, *Leadership is Male*,[39] captures accurately what complementarians believe: men are to lead, women submit, the patriarchal principle.

Note, I said I was giving the complementarian position in "plain English." In complementarian literature as a general rule everything is said in code language. The position is put in euphemistic and obfuscating wording to sound acceptable to the modern ear. The self-designation, the "complementarian position," is a classic example. All Christians should believe God has made us male and female and the two sexes *complete* what it means to be human. If complementarians wanted to accurately self-designate their position to reflect what they teach it should be called the "hierarchical" view of the sexes, or "biblical patriarchy." Possibly their most egregious corruption of language is seen in their insistence that "we teach the equality of the sexes," even the "absolute equality" of the sexes.[40] However, what they are affirming is not social equality, substantive

---

38. Anglican Diocese of Sydney, "Responding."

39. Pawson, *Leadership is Male*.

40. Hartley, "Evolution of the Gender Debate," 6, column 2, line 16. See also the Sydney website, "Equal but Different," for the same words.

equality, but spiritual equality, or equality before God, that has no social implications in this world. In their thinking some are *more equal* than others! Men lead, women submit. "Difference" is another code word. For complementarians, what defines a man as a man is that he leads, and what defines a woman as a woman is that she is submissive to the men set over her. When complementarians hear egalitarian evangelicals deny this difference, they accuse them of denying difference itself.[41] No evangelical egalitarian denies that God has indelibly differentiated the sexes by giving them different bodies and chromosomes. If two things are identical, we say they are "the same." The word difference in contrast says two things that are different in some ways are to be considered as equal in some ways. The word "role" is another code word. Instead of saying men are to rule, women submit, we are told "men and women are equal, they simply have been given different *roles*." What are these differing "roles"? Men have the leading "role"; women the submitting "role." In this cryptic wording, a "role" refers to the differing power given to men and women that can never change, *not* as we would expect if we were following dictionary usage, characteristic behavior that can change.[42]

In opposition stand those who call themselves "evangelical egalitarians," who argue the Bible clearly makes the substantial equality of the sexes the God-given ideal. They hold that in creation before the fall, God bestowed on the man and the woman the same status, dignity, and leadership ability (Gen 1:27–28); the rule of the man over the woman is entirely a consequence of the fall (Gen 3:16), and is thus an expression of sin, and this is exactly what Jesus believed. The few texts in the New Testament that speak of the subordination of women or wives, like those to slaves, are simply practical advice to those living in a culture that took for granted the subordination of women and the institution of slavery. In my 2018 book, *What the Bible Actually Teaches on Women*, I outline this position in full and deconstruct the complementarian position. So far no one has made a reply.

41. This is a constant charge made in the classic exposition of the complementarian position by Köstenberger and Köstenberger, *God's Design*, 162, 165, 195, 311, etc.

42. Another hidden truth is that for complementarian theology, the man is set over the woman in creation before the fall. This must mean that in all of creation, society, the church and the home, men are to rule over women. This was generally believed what the Bible taught until the twentieth century. Today complementarians say we are only arguing that men are set over women in the church and the home, something contrary to their own appeal to the pre-fall creation order.

Evangelical egalitarians read the Bible as a liberating message. Jesus Christ came into the world "to set the oppressed free" (Luke 4:18). They take anything in the Bible that could be read to set men over women as nothing more than a reflection of the world in which the biblical writers lived. First-century Christians assumed that the sun revolved around the earth, slavery was acceptable to God, and women were subordinated to men. Twenty-first-century Christians should not believe these things and need not. What they are bound to believe is what the Bible *teaches*. As far as men and women are concerned, they are bound to believe that God made man and woman alike in his image, giving them alike the mandate to rule over his world (Gen 1:27–28), that the fall is the basis for women's subordinate status (Gen 3:16)—a reflection of sin to be opposed by Christians—and that Jesus said not one word that would suggest men are set over women, and much to the contrary, and that abuse and violence are always displeasing to Jesus Christ.

Now I return to the question, "What causes, or better, 'drives,' *some* Christian men to abuse the woman they say they love?" The answer must be it is the same causes or drivers that lead non-Christian men to abuse their wife or partner. Primary is a belief in male entitlement, the conviction that men are born to lead, women to follow, exactly what complementarians teach, and secondary are wounds in the psyche and in the thinking of individual men—a feeling of powerlessness as a man, an awareness that anger can get what you want, and possibly the experience of abuse by your father of your mother. These inner forces determine how abusive behavior by any one man is expressed. What is added for Christians is that it is possible for them to appeal to the Bible in support of their determination to be in charge, to make all the important decisions and to insist that their wife be submissive. And this is just what virtually all abusers in our churches do. They think the Bible encourages them to be strong leaders in the home, to have the final say on all important matters, and that their wife or partner should be submissive "in all things," as St. Paul says (Eph 5:24).[43]

Complementarians consistently and loudly reject the claim that the Bible can encourage and legitimate abuse and violence in the home. They often say, "the least likely group [of men] to engage in domestic violence" are those who attend evangelical churches regularly,[44] or even that male

---

43. I have heard this said countless times.

44. And conversely, that men "who are irregular church attendees are the most likely to batter their wives." So, Tracy, "Patriarchy and Domestic Abuse," and Wilcox,

headship is "good for women, good for children, and good for families."[45] As I mentioned earlier, at the annual Southern Baptist Convention meeting in Dallas in 2018, where some 8,000 delegates were present, a resolution was passed, condemning domestic abuse, asserting that headship teaching "neither supports nor fosters, but rather prevents and condemns abuse."[46] Similarly, Mark Thompson, the principal of Moore Theological College, Sydney says, "Biblical headship and submission is not the cause [of domestic abuse], *in fact quite the opposite.*"[47]

The problem for complementarians is that these assertions are patently false. In recent years, innumerable Christian women have come forward to say unambiguously in one way or another something like, "My husband believes God has put him in charge of our home and I must submit to him. He believes it is his job to discipline me. He always quotes the Bible in support." In every book or article I read on abuse in churchgoing homes, women are quoted as saying her abusive and violent husband constantly appealed to scriptural teaching on headship and wifely submission to justify his behavior. In all my personal encounters with abusive men in my many years as a pastor, every one of them quoted the Bible in support of their behavior. Of all the reading I did in preparing to write this book, none more eloquently told the story of how biblical teaching on male headship and female submission can encourage and legitimate abuse by a Christian husband, in this case an evangelical pastor, than Ruth Tucker's *Black and White Bible, Black and Blue Wife—My Story of Finding Hope After Domestic Abuse.*[48] She says her pastor husband whenever he was in a violent rage "hurled texts at me, as though the principal tenet in Scripture was, 'Wives submit to your husbands.'"

"Evangelicals and Domestic Abuse." Complementarians repeat this argument incessantly. It has no validity whatsoever. Regular churchgoing men are in fact serious offenders. Furthermore, at least in Australia and Europe, there are very few irregular male church attenders, and even less who quote the Bible to justify their behavior. Most telling is that two social scientists, Naomi Priest and Nicolas Biddle, evaluated the studies Tracy and Wilcox base their claim on and found that they did not support their conclusions. See Priest and Biddle, "Verdict on Domestic Violence Data."

45. Moore, "After Patriarchy, What?" 576.

46. "On Abuse." I thank Denny Burk for referring me to this resolution.

47. Anglican Diocese of Sydney, "Responding," 51. Italics added.

48. Tucker, *Black and White Bible.*

Headship Teaching and Abuse

At this point of time there is no avoiding the fact that there is a relationship between domestic abuse and violence and biblical teaching on the headship of men and the submission of women. Scholarly studies on domestic abuse and violence are agreed that the primary driver of this scourge is a sense of male entitlement; the belief that men should lead simply because they are men, and women should be submissive simply because they are women. Let me quote again, "Change the Story": "Research has consistently found that men who hold traditional, hierarchical views about gender roles and relationships are more likely to perpetuate violence against women."[49] And *The Lancet*, "The main drivers of partner violence are gender related norms and hierarchies that shape relationships between men and women."[50] And lastly, Stephen Tracy, "Models of patriarchy which give husbands the greatest levels of power and authority are most likely to stimulate domestic abuse.[51]

In this last quote, Professor Tracy implicitly identifies Christian headship teaching as a form of patriarchy. Most complementarians avoid this term, wanting, as we have noted, to put their position in more obfuscating and euphemistic wording. However, many of the most-informed and most-able complementarian theologians agree with Tracy. The complementarian position may accurately be called, "Christian or biblical patriarchy." It holds that men should be in charge and make all the important decisions and women are to be submissive. Denny Burk, the chairman of the Council for Biblical Manhood and Womanhood, the flagship of the complementarian movement, says, "Biblical patriarchy isn't such a bad designation. It is simply what the Scriptures teach about manhood and womanhood."[52] Joe Carter, the editor of The Gospel Coalition website, a widely read complementarian blog, says, complementarians "must not fear making a claim that is disturbingly counter cultural . . . Christianity is undergirded by a vision of patriarchy." He then adds that patriarchy is not a negative term for "those of us who serve the God of Abraham, Isaac, and Jacob—the God and Father of Jesus Christ."[53] Russell Moore, the

---

49. "Change the Story," 25.

50. Heise and Kotsadam, "Cross-National and Multilevel Correlates of Partner Violence," 336. This is put as a thesis to be tested. It is found correct by the research.

51. Tracy, "Asking Christians to Do Better."

52. Burk, "Complementarianism or Patriarchy?

53. Carter, "Debatable."

president of the Southern Baptist Convention Ethics and Religious Liberty Commission, could not be more forthright. For him, authentic complementarian teaching is biblically prescribed, and rightly called, "Christian patriarchy." God has appointed men to lead in the church and the home and women need to respect their leadership.[54] For most complementarians, Andreas and Margaret Köstenberger's 2014 book, *God's Design for Men and Women,* is taken as the most scholarly and up-to-date exposition of their position.[55] They argue that patriarchy is normative for the Bible where it is seen as "benevolent and beneficial rather than intrinsically abusive or oppressive."[56] However, they say, in today's world this term is all too often viewed negatively and so they tell us they prefer the term *"patricentric"* to designate what they think is the biblical view of the family and the one they endorse. This term literally means, so they say, "father-centeredness,"[57] or more generally, I add, man-centeredness. In opting for this term, we are left with no uncertainty about their beliefs.

Now let me put what we have learnt in sharp and blunt terms. Leading complementarian theologians agree that complementarian theology may rightly be called, "Christian patriarchy." Patriarchy and complementarianism are both predicated on the belief that men should lead and women be submissive. The problem with this is that virtually all the scholarly studies on domestic abuse and violence agree that the patriarchal premise, men should lead, making all the important decisions, and women should be submissive, is the most consistent predictor of violence against women.

If the abuse of women is to be effectively countered this belief in male privilege and female submission has to be rejected. Carrie Yodanis says for more than thirty years scholars have agreed that,

> In order to stop men's use and women's experience of violence on the personal level, structures of gender inequality at the societal level must change. . . . Gender inequality, or patriarchy, is both ideological (the beliefs, norms, and values about the status and roles of women in society) and structural (women's access to positions of leadership within social institutions).[58]

54. Moore, "After Patriarchy, What?" 569–76, quotes from 576.

55. See the 18 glowing endorsements on the first pages of the book by the best-known and most-informed complementarians.

56. Köstenberger and Köstenberger, *God's Design,* 60.

57. Köstenberger and Köstenberger, *God's Design,* 60.

58. Yodanis, "Gender Inequality," 58.

If this is so, and complementarians really want to effectively counter domestic abuse and violence in their homes and in their churches, then the challenge before them is clear and unambiguous. "To stop men's use and women's experience of violence on the personal level, structures of gender inequality at the societal level must change."[59] To achieve this noble goal, complementarians have to give up teaching men should lead and women be "submissive" in the home and the church.

The Happy Marriage Today

Every man or woman who attends a church with a complementarian pastor would have heard headship teaching many times. Such pastors, as a general rule, love to teach on this topic. Nevertheless, most men in churches where complementarian teaching is regularly given, do not in any concrete way practice what is preached in their homes. If they have a happy and mutually rewarding marriage, they are in practice egalitarians. For them, headship teaching is a notional idea (just in the head) and nothing more. In today's world, a "happy marriage" is by definition a profoundly equal relationship. Some honest complementarian leaders admit that they have fully equal marriages, and that most complementarian couples have such equal marriages![60] Russell Moore, the Southern Baptist leader, says that most Christian marriages, including those who call themselves complementarians, are "pragmatically egalitarian."[61] In these marriages, headship teaching has been emptied of "its authoritative character."[62] The Sydney Anglican theologian and defender of the complementarian position, Michael Jensen, speaking specifically of fellow complementarian clergy in Sydney, says all their "marriages are remarkably egalitarian."[63] This he sees as highly commendable! But whether or not complementarians openly confess that in most cases their marriages are profoundly equal, one cannot miss the fact that if a couple obviously have a happy and mutually rewarding marriage it is largely an equal one, and if the marriage is fraught very often the husband is seeking to exert his power over his wife—or she over him. What this

---

59. Yodanis, "Gender Inequality," 58.

60. This is the substance of Moore's article, "After Patriarchy, What?" He is a dogmatic complementarian.

61. Moore, "After Patriarchy, What?," 571.

62. Moore, "After Patriarchy, What?," 573.

63. Jensen, *Sydney Anglicanism,* 140.

means is that even in churches where male headship is frequently preached, claiming this is "what the Bible clearly teaches," most of the marriages are fully equal relationships. Couples hear this teaching, but it is not how they operate. This means headship teaching in no way tempts them to abuse or be violent to their wives.

The problem is that *some* men in churches where complementarian teaching is part of the stable sermon diet, hear this teaching and seek to apply it literally. They insist on being in control and making all the major decisions. They tell their wives that they should be submissive and obey them. They hear their pastor saying, "You are a man, you should be in charge, you should make all the important decisions; to be a man is to be strong, powerful and in control."[64] On this basis, they seek to get their own way by verbal abuse, threats, anger, quoting the Bible, and sometimes violence—holding their fist up, slapping, choking, poking, throwing, and hitting. When they feel they are losing control they make sure they win. For such men headship teaching is toxic.

You would hope that the example of Jesus who always related to women as he did to men, and who taught us to love our neighbor as our self, would counter any inclination in a Christian man to abuse his wife. However, none can deny there is abuse in the homes of *some* couples who regularly go to church, and in the homes of some clergy/pastors, especially in the homes of members of evangelical, Reformed, and Pentecostal churches where headship teaching is common. We have just seen the reason for this. Needy and controlling men hear headship teaching as encouraging and justifying their behavior. They sincerely believe that God wants them to rule in their home; God wants them to be a "real man" who is respected and is rightly in control of his own family, the one who makes all the big decisions, who makes sure that his wife does what Scripture commands—"wives be submissive to your husband in all things" (Eph 5:24, Col 2:18), and like Sarah be "obedient" to your husband (1 Pet 3:6).[65] Complementarians may say *ad infinitum* that nothing in the Bible could in any way encourage or legitimate the abuse of one's wife, but nothing is more common in the homes of churchgoers where abuse is present than appeals to the Bible by men in support of their actions.

64. See Hill, *See What You Made Me Do,* 115.

65. Like Eph 5:22–33, 1 Pet 3:1–6 is difficult for all modern-day Christians because not only does it ask women to obey their husbands but also it can be read to tell women to hang in there even if their husband is violent. See my discussion of this text in chapter 4 of this book.

At this point we should see the stark contrast. Abusive men in the community at large, who are not church attenders, must make up excuses for their awful behavior. Men who are regular church attenders, especially those well-versed in complementarian teaching, can, and frequently do, appeal to the Bible to justify their behavior. They feel they are acting in a way pleasing to God. They are asserting their authority as real men. Their wives should respect them and do as they expect. If wives do not, then the husband needs to remind them that they are rejecting "the clear teaching of Scripture." This "biblical" justification of abuse gives to the Christian abuser power that the non-churchgoer abuser can never have. The Christian abuser believes he has divine approval for the way he acts in his home. This is why headship teaching is so damaging for many churchgoing men and women.

The fact is that headship teaching in our churches has had direful consequences for too many Christian women. It has led to them being sinned against. Surely this should make all complementarians critically think about their appeals to Scripture to support male headship and female submission as what is pleasing to God. Can this teaching be pleasing to God if all too often it blights Christian marriages?

Now to Be Perfectly Fair

At this point, I must add that complementarians *today* with one voice loudly condemn domestic abuse and violence. This is a repeated refrain in everything they say on this very difficult issue for them. I could fill the next two pages with very forceful condemnations by complementarians of domestic abuse and violence *in the last ten years*. The problem for them is that the evidence is now in; teaching that men should be in charge, make all the major decisions and women should be submissive "in all things" can encourage and legitimate abuse in needy and controlling men, and such men are found in every church and among the clergy. Saying in a loud voice, time and time again, that headship teaching "properly explained" does not have this consequence does not advance the discussion one iota. The fact is that too many churchgoing men, including too many pastors, take headship teaching to be saying, "You men should be in charge; your wife should obey and respect your decisions."

In the face of the overwhelming evidence that the belief that men should lead and women be submissive is the primary driver in domestic abuse and violence, what complementarians need to do, and seem unable to do, is consider afresh whether or not the Bible makes the headship of men and the submission of women the creation ideal and thus what is pleasing to God. Evangelical egalitarians have answered in the negative, complementarians seem unable to even consider the question.

Preaching Headship, a Form of Abuse

In churches with a complementarian pastor, headship teaching as a usual rule gets a lot of airspace. Numerous church members over the years have told me that their pastor comes back to this topic time and time again. It seems, they say, that "for him, nothing in the whole Bible is more important than the headship of the man and the submission of women." One of my readers who has belonged to a Sydney Anglican Church for most of her life wrote back to me on reading these words, saying,

> My experience is a bit different. Our minister each year has a month-long series of sermons on "the Christian family." In these sermons we hear a lot about male headship and female submission, why women should minister only to other women and children, and why men only should be ordained and preach.

For all complementarians, the headship/leadership of men and the submission of women is not just an opinion; it is "what the Bible clearly teaches." To be told week after week that the Bible clearly teaches God has put men in charge and women should be submissive places a huge burden on the conscience of every church member. Who wants to directly disbelieve and disobey what the preacher dogmatically says "is what the Bible clearly teaches"?

For many Christian women, well-educated, holding very responsible jobs, and living in a world where women are prime ministers, state premiers or governors, mayors, judges, lawyers, doctors, professors, airline pilots, etc., this teaching is profoundly discordant with their life outside of the church and in most cases with how their marriage works. They find this teaching offensive, demeaning, and *abusive*, and research shows that in large numbers they have left the church. This teaching certainly hinders evangelism among women and blights church membership for many women and men.

If this teaching on male headship and female submission as the God-given creation ideal is in fact *not* what the Bible clearly teaches, then these pastors are being spiritually abusive. They are exalting men and putting down women, claiming divine sanction for what they preach, when they know that large numbers of evangelical and Reformed theologians are of a counter opinion.[66] These "egalitarian evangelical" theologians argue that the Bible makes the substantial equality of the sexes the God-given ideal; the rule of the man over the woman is entirely a consequence of the fall (Gen 3:16). It is an expression of sin.[67] If pastors of complementarian conviction honestly and openly admitted that many of the best-known and most-able evangelical biblical scholars disagreed with their teaching, we might excuse their many sermons on male headship/leadership and female submission, but they do not. They insist that this is "what the Bible clearly teaches" and anyone who disagrees with them does not accept the authority of Scripture, implying that they are not true Christians. This would not be such a serious problem if teaching male headship and female submission did not have such awful consequences for so many Christian women.

What is Needed is Balanced Preaching

Paul undeniably says just once, "the man is the head of his wife," and twice he asks wives to be submissive/subordinate to their husbands, but what about the cultural and literary context in which he wrote these words? Immediately prior to saying that the husband is the head of his wife (Eph 5:23), the cultural norm of his day, Paul asks husbands and wives to submit to each other (Eph 5:21), and immediately after (Eph 5: 25–33), husbands to love their wives to the point of giving his life for her—ideas that are entirely novel and distinctively Christian. Why not concentrate on these verses where we find a profoundly equal understanding of marriage? I will say more on Eph 5:21–33 in chapter 4. And why not speak often and long on 1 Cor 7:1–39 where Paul makes marriage a fully equal and reciprocal relationship, saying not one word on male headship? And why not preach often on Jesus and marriage? We are followers of Jesus, and so was Paul. Our Lord said not one word on male headship and wifely submission and much to the contrary.

66. In my *What the Bible Actually Teaches on Women* I list some of these scholars, see xvi n. 9, 25–26.

67. I set this case out in great detail in *What the Bible Actually Teaches.*

And why never speak on domestic abuse and violence? I have not heard one sermon on this topic and I expect this is the experience of most church-goers. This is a surprising omission by evangelical pastors who say their aim is to preach the whole counsel of God as it is revealed in Scripture. The Bible says God hates abuse and violence (Jud 19:5; Ps 11:5; 140:11; Prov 6:17; Jer 7:6; 22:3; Ezek 7:11; 8:17; Amos 3:10; Mic 6:8–12; and probably Mal 2:17; etc.) And, the Bible condemns leaders of God's people who do not stand up for and protect the vulnerable and the weak (Ps 10:1–18; Prov 24:11–12; Isa 1:17; 3:14–25; Jer 22:3, 13–19; Zech 7:10; Jas 5:2–6; etc.).

And lastly, I ask, why do pastors not preach often on the joy and re-wards of a fully equal marriage, instead of the headship model? If they are happily married, this is their experience and delight. Why seek to impose a patriarchal view of marriage on couples living in the twenty-first cen-tury that has nothing to commend it and all too often makes marriages unhappy, even abusive?

Chapter 3

The Abuse of Women in the Developing World

THE STATISTICS ON DOMESTIC abuse and violence in the developed world, as we have outlined them, are appalling. In the developing world they are much worse. Women suffer in many ways simply because they are women. Nicolas Kristoff and Sheryl WuDunn say, "the global statistics are numbing."[1]

> It appears that more women have been killed in the last fifty years, precisely because they were women, than men were killed in all the battles of the twentieth century. More women are killed in this routine "gendercide" in any one decade than people were slaughtered in all the genocides of the twentieth century.[2]

Should any one wish to hear more of this tragic story, the book to read is Elaine Storkey's *Scars Across Humanity*. I have read nothing quite like it. Her book is a graphic account of the violence inflicted on women in today's world. The book is very well researched, accessible, and spine chilling. As I sat with the book in hand, I felt both pleased that someone had so powerfully told this horrible story and depressed by what I was reading. After an introductory chapter, the following eight chapters deal with specific forms of violence against women in the chronological order that they are most likely to occur in a woman's life: the abortion of female fetuses and infanticide, genital mutilation, early forced marriage, honor killing, domestic abuse, trafficking and prostitution, rape, and attacks in war.

Jimmy Carter says that economic disparity between the developing world and the developed world is a huge and growing problem but he says,

---

1. Kristoff and WuDunn, *Half the Sky*, xvi.
2. Kristoff and WuDunn, *Half the Sky*, xvi.

"I have become convinced that *the most serious and unaddressed worldwide challenge is the deprivation and abuse of women and girls.*"[3]

Ronald Sider says the marginalization, devaluing and dehumanizing of half of the population in the developing world leads to:

- a preference for boys that results in tens of millions of aborted female fetuses;
- inequality in education for women;
- inequality in health for women;
- inequality in ownership of property and work for women;
- inequality in income for women;
- widespread and accepted violence against women;
- the trafficking of women, primarily for prostitution.[4]

Why Does This Happen to Women?

Jimmy Carter is in no doubt. He says the widespread discrimination against and abuse of women around the world is "based on the presupposition that men and boys are superior to women and girls."[5]

Elaine Storkey agrees but she is more expansive. She says at the lowest level of explanation, men abuse women simply because they can.[6] They are more powerful socially, politically, and physically. And in most religious societies, their holy texts legitimate the exercise of male power over women: patriarchy. She says, patriarchy is a complex social phenomenon which affects both men and women. It is based on a pervasive set of beliefs that brainwash men and women into believing that the male domination of women is beneficial when there is no evidence of this. It is in fact a dangerous myth that cripples both men and women. Women are always treated badly when men believe that they are privileged, they should be in charge and make all the important decisions.[7]

3. Carter, *Call to Action*, 3.
4. Sider, "Gender and Justice."
5. Carter, *Call to Action*, 4.
6. Storkey, *Scars Across Humanity*, 170.
7. Storkey, *Scars Across Humanity*, 181–86.

In every country in the world, the post-1960s emancipation of women, basically a Western phenomenon, has had some impact, but in many developing countries the response has been reactionary. It has been sharply opposed. Little progress has been made in advancing the welfare of women. We see the huge challenges facing women in the developing world in noting that more than 603 million women live in countries where domestic violence is not a crime and not likely to be any time in the near future.[8]

Domestic Abuse and Violence

The 2013 World Health Organization Report, "Violence Against Women," states that domestic violence against women is pervasive globally. It is a world-wide public health problem of epidemic proportions, requiring urgent action. The researchers say the global prevalence of physical and/or sexual intimate partner violence among all ever-partnered women is 30.0 percent. The prevalence is higher in African, Eastern Mediterranean, and South-East Asia regions, where approximately 37 percent of ever-partnered women reported having experienced physical and/or sexual intimate partner violence. This report also makes the point that situations of political conflict, post conflict, and displacement exacerbate violence by intimate partners as well as physical and sexual violence more generally. I quote these figures from the summary of the WHO report, which are certainly very conservative. In the full report, figures from specific locations are given. In these we are told that 45.6 percent of women in many African nations have experienced intimate partner abuse, 40.2 percent in South East Asia, and in India the estimated figures are even higher.[9] Women and girls with disabilities are by far the most vulnerable.

Where abuse and violence is endemic, women internalize their subordinate status and almost take it for granted that they will be beaten. A UNICEF report, based on a survey of women aged fifteen to forty-nine, revealed that 90 percent of wives in Afghanistan and Jordan, 86 percent in Mali, 86 percent in Guinea and Timor-Leste, 81 percent in Laos, and 80 percent in the Central African Republic believed that a husband is justified in hitting or beating his wife under certain circumstances.[10]

---

8. Storkey, *Scars Across Humanity*, 77.

9. See World Health Organization, "Violence Against Women," 16.

10. Carter, *Call to Action*, 143.

Seeing is Believing

My wife Lynley and I have traveled widely in the Middle East, India, South East Asia, and Africa. We have seen with our own eyes the things the World Health Organization discusses and what Ron Sider describes. We know it is true that where men are privileged and women devalued, women come off very badly.

I have traveled to the Philippines with Lynley three times, once with World Vision on development work, twice as a visiting lecturer at the Asian Theological Seminary in Quezon City. While waiting to preach at a large Baptist church in Manilla, the pastor said to me,

> Kevin, you will see about twenty smartly dressed young women sitting together at the back of the church. They are prostitutes. Sunday mornings are quiet so they get a couple of hours off. Their poor fathers sold them when they were about 10 years old to the brothel owner. We do all we can for them and help them if they escape but it is not easy. If they run away, they have nowhere to go. Their family will not take them back and if they are caught, they will be beaten and possibly killed.

India

Let me tell another story. In 2007 Lynley and I spent a month in India. I was invited to be a plenary speaker at an Indian Christians for Biblical Equality (CBE) conference and to lecture at the South Asian Institute of Advanced Christian Studies, both in Bangalore. India has possibly the highest incidence of abuse of women in the world. It is estimated that 70 percent of women have been subject to domestic abuse. In addition, it has the highest incidence of rape and murder of women. 65 percent of men believe women should accept violence at the hand of their husband to keep the family together and often women deserve to be beaten.[11] In the churches, traditional Indian beliefs about women and marriage tend to be reflected. We were told that most pastors preach the doctrine of male headship: men should be the leader in the home and make all the important decisions and the wife should be submissive and obedient. This was understood to be clear biblical endorsement for the prevailing and

---

11. "Violence Against Women in India." Deepa, "India's Abuse of Women," says, "India's abuse of women is the biggest human rights violation on earth."

traditional hierarchical ordering of the sexes. Not surprisingly, we were told that abuse is very common in Indian Christian homes.

At the CBE conference, several very able Indian men and women were speakers. They all made the point that the multi-faceted abuse of women in Indian society was present in the church and that both the Hindu Scriptures and the Christian Scriptures could be quoted in support of a high view of women *and* of their subordination to men, with the latter getting the most air space. The great challenge for egalitarian evangelical theologians in India, we were told, was to convince pastors that the Bible makes the substantial equality of the sexes the creation-given ideal and the subordination of women is entirely a consequence of the fall, and that Jesus said not one word on male headship and the submission of women, and much to the contrary. This was an uphill battle because most of the pastors had been trained by Western evangelical academics who had taught them that male headship and female submission were "what the Bible clearly taught." To affirm the equality of the two sexes would demand the changing of their theology.

In our travels in India we saw much evidence on how badly women were treated as a consequence of their lowly status. When we came back to Australia, we decided to make at least a small gesture by sponsoring two Indian girls through World Vision. Both girls' parents had never been to school. We have their photos on our fridge and we hope and pray for a better future for them.

Africa

In 2018, Lynley and I were invited by three different Christian "non-profits" or "Non-Government Organizations" (NGOs) to speak mainly to pastors and their wives on marriage at conferences in South Africa, Kenya, and Uganda. Those who organized our trip invited us to speak against abuse and violence in Christian homes. We declined; we said we needed to begin on the positive—what makes a marriage rewarding for both the man and the woman, what fosters love and what destroys love. They agreed.

What we learned of the extent of the abuse and violence in African Christian homes in general, and in clergy couples in particular, left us dumbfounded. People were amazingly honest and open about this matter. It soon became evident that three powerful forces were at work. First, in much of Africa, a man or his family have to pay a bride price for a wife and this is often a hefty sum, or the equivalent in livestock. In South Africa, a taxi driver told us he wanted 20,000 Rand (the price of a new medium-sized car) for his daughter whom he had educated through high school and university. The problem is that when a man "buys" his wife in this way, he thinks he owns her and she is his lifetime servant.

Second, African culture is profoundly patriarchal. It is believed men should be in charge and women should do as they are told by their husband. If they do not, they will certainly be verbally abused and often "disciplined"—which was a nice word for hit, bashed, or beaten.

Third, in much of sub-Saharan Africa, Christianity is the predominant religion and the churches are well attended. In most of the churches, headship teaching is emphasized and is frequently a topic of sermons.

When wives are seen as possessions and the culture says men should be in charge in all spheres of life and the pastors teach that men should be the leaders and women submissive, we have fertile ground for abuse to flourish—and it does.

We went to Uganda at the invitation of the Reverend Patti Ricotta, the president and co-founder of *Life Together International*. She has been working among the Sabiny people in Eastern Uganda for seven years. They were first evangelized in the late nineteenth and early twentieth centuries by Anglican missionaries. The wonderful response we received was in large part due to her preparatory work. In all her teaching, she had stressed that the Bible teaches the equal value, dignity, and ability of men and women. At first, she applied this teaching in opposition to female genital mutilation, a cultural practice of the Sabiny people, and many other African cultures, and she has seen it almost eliminated. She invited Lynley and me because the clergy she had been working with asked her for someone to speak to them on how equal marriages worked.

In our three-day conference in the regional city of Kapchorwa, about 150 Sabiny Anglican ministers and their wives were present (total of about 300). After we had been introduced, the very first question one pastor asked was, "Will all the clergy get a certificate to say they had been trained as marriage counselors by Kevin and Lynley Giles?" We saw many heads nodding. I asked what they thought marriage counseling is all about. The questioner said, "Knowing what to say when wives come to us complaining about their husband, or what to tell husbands when they are having trouble with their wife." It seemed to us that some clergy agreed with him, others did not. Lynley then came in and said, "Marriage counseling by definition is couple counseling. You listen to both parties, seeking to hear and understand what each person is saying and feeling." We could see not everyone in the room agreed with what she had said. Sensing this, the questioner tried again. He said, "I don't do that. I think it's up to the man to say what the problem is, or problems are, in the marriage. The Bible says the man is the head of the home and the wife should obey him. Most of the problems in our marriages are caused by the women who won't do as they are told." At this point Lynley said,

> It's good to hear how you see things but we are here to explore with you ways that might make your marriages work much better and how you pastors might counsel in a much more productive way. We are not here to train you as counselors; we are here to help you as couples to have a better marriage. No certificates in counseling will be given out.

From day one, it was very clear that for most of those present their marriages were not working. The women were very unhappy and the men knew this. Several times men asked, "Why do our wives not want to have sex with us?" The pastors had heard from Patti about marriage equality, and they were very open to this idea, but they did not know how to put it into practice. They had not seen marriages where equality prevailed. They simply had no idea how this could operate or what it would look like. It seemed to Lynley and me there was more willingness to change than we had ever seen in Western pastors. This of course was due to Patti Ricotta's seven years of ministry among them.

In our presentations, Lynley and I spoke dialogically. One would begin, speaking for say five minutes and then the other would speak, often commenting on what had just been said and then adding to this. In an introductory talk we spoke of how our marriage had changed and evolved over fifty years. We openly told them that in Australia and other Western countries virtually every "happy" marriage was a profoundly equal one. Our age gave us a lot of respect. They listened attentively. In another talk, we discussed what *agapē*/love involved in a marriage, going through 1 Corinthians chapter 13, a section at a time. And we tackled Eph 5:21–33, making the point that what is distinctively Christian and revolutionary in this text is the exhortation to mutual subordination and the demand that husbands love their wives like Christ loved the church and gave his life for it. The way we presented unsettled our audience and caught their attention. They had never heard a husband and wife share like this and do so in harmony. I suspect what we did was more powerful than what we said.

Despite the huge challenges we faced, we got an amazing response. Near the end, Lynley spent an hour or more with about a hundred Ugandan pastors' wives and virtually all of them said how unhappy they were in their marriages. (I met with the men who only wanted to talk theology!) In the plenary session following, which concluded the conference, Lynley told the men how unhappy their wives were. She told them vividly what they had said about doing all the work, their husband spending too much money on himself, speaking rudely to them and often hitting them, and commonly taking a second wife (a woman "on the side"). There was deadly silence except for a few men crying. Then one senior pastor, a well-educated man, stood up and said,

> I came on the first day on my own to see what it was all about and then spent the night talking to my wife about our marriage. She and I have come each day since then. For the first time I have seen how selfish and cruel I have been. I thought the Bible taught God had put me in charge in my home and my wife should do as I told her. I had bought her; she was my servant. The result has been we have been very unhappy in our marriage. I stand to ask my wife for forgiveness and I promise to change.

It was as if the air had been sucked out of the room. Then, one after another, men stood up to say something similar. The consensus in the room was that headship teaching, as interpreted in their culture, had led men to be very selfish and often abusive of their wives and had driven love and enriching sexual intimacy out the door. They needed to listen to the Bible afresh. One pastor stood and said,

> Kevin and Lynley, you have shown us that in creation God gave the same dignity, status and leadership abilities to men and women. Jesus said not one word on male headship and insisted that leadership in his family is all about lowly humble service. St Paul made mutual subordination in marriage and the costly self-giving of the husband the essence of a Christian marriage. Patti has taught us this but its so good to hear you and Lynley say the same and show us how it is done.

There were nods all around the room. Then another man stood and said,

> Patti had told us this, but when you as a man said this, Kevin, and we saw how it worked with you and Lynley, the light went on.

When we were back in Australia, Patti wrote to us to thank us for our ministry. She gave me permission to use her words.

> When you two talked about how your relationship had evolved over the years to the point where now the best part is your companionship—doing things together and being like-minded—it made a huge impact on those present. I thought it was the most important lessons these couples could learn. I personally was astounded to see how much this meant to everyone there and how it made so many couples, especially the men, choose to think about how you achieved this in 50 years being happily married. Do you remember how several clergy said that many, many marriages among the Sabiny and other African groups, end after the childbearing years because the woman can't stand to be with the domineering husband anymore? Many women go to live with one of their children to get away from him and the man is left all alone in his elder years, sad and depressed. It had never occurred to them that a couple could stay together happily for 50 years—like you have—if they would only live the way you described, in mutual respect, enjoying each other's company. They recognized the great contrast between the beauty and rewards of your marriage, and the ugliness and pain of so many of their marriages where the man wanted everything his own way and treated his wife as a servant.

On reading Ruth Tucker's powerful book, *Black and White Bible, Black and Blue Wife,* I discovered she had twice taught courses at Moffat Bible College in Kenya and had suffered much the same cultural shock that we had on hearing Christian men defend "wife beating. . . . if she deserved it."[12]

The Sudanese

Australia has welcomed about 20,000 Sudanese refugees in the last thirty years, the highest number having come to Victoria, my home state. The overwhelming majority of them identify as Christians and they go to church regularly. I have had quite a bit to do with members of this community. Lynley and I sponsored two young Sudanese men at different times, both of whom we saw married. We would not have taken this on if we had realized what a big responsibility and time-consuming exercise this would be. Refugees face many challenges and difficulties in their new home country. Later, I tutored one morning a week for two years, ten Sudanese men studying

12. Tucker, *Black and White Bible*, 117.

at university or seminary who wanted to improve their spoken and written English. And most recently we both gave considerable time to helping a Sudanese couple with seven children. He is a clergyman.

Without a shadow of doubt, the hardest thing for Sudanese men coming to a developed country like Australia is the equality of women. Theirs is a profoundly patriarchal society where women do virtually all the work, are expected to have six or seven children and have no rights. In my English classes, every morning almost without exception, they began with a discussion on something to do with women in Australia. All these men saw themselves as Christians and belonged to a church community. One thing that really upset them is that besides government unemployment benefits and housing rent assistance paid into their joint account, most if not all of them were getting the government paid child support benefit. Every Australian family with children under 18 gets this, which the Australian government wisely pays directly into an account in the mother's name only. With six, seven, or eight children this is worth over $4,000 a month. All the men hated this policy. They said the money should go to them. It was insulting for a man to have ask his wife for money for his car, or a new computer, or to buy drinks for his friends. They said it just causes conflict. This matter came up time and time again but nothing I said could convince them of the wisdom of this policy. For them, it was clear, men should control all money in the home.

One morning, before the English lesson began, one Sudanese student said to me, "Kevin can I tell you what happened last night?" I said, "Sure but be brief as I want to get onto our English lesson." He said,

> Last night when I got home from university, the evening meal was not ready and I found the house in a mess. I got angry with my wife, raised my voice and pushed her against the wall. I didn't hurt her. The next thing I know is there is a knock on the door and when I opened it, I found two policemen standing there. They asked me a few questions and I admitted that I had sworn at my wife and pushed her against the wall. With that they asked me to come with them to the police station and there they charged me with the abuse of my wife. They assumed it was my fault. They would not listen to my argument that my wife was to blame. This is certainly a strange country where a woman is listened to, not her husband.

I noted that all the other men were nodding their heads.

Domestic abuse and violence in Sudanese homes in Australia is a huge problem. Every one of the men I have got to know has had problems with this. Too commonly, Sudanese men believe they should be obeyed and women need to be "disciplined" if they do not do as they are told. The clergy couple I mentioned above broke up after he hit her repeatedly and finally bit her.

The other thing that I learnt is that Sudanese men expect their wives to do all the work. Frequently in documentaries telling of food drops to Sudanese villages in this war-torn country, you see the women carrying off the large bags of aid grain on their heads as the men watch. I learnt this lesson early when I asked the first of the two young Sudanese men we sponsored to dry the dishes after the welcoming meal we had put on for him in our home. He said, "Sudanese men do not do housework." An interesting discussion followed but he would not pick up a tea towel. More than twenty years later the Sudanese clergy couple I mentioned above asked if anyone in the church would help them move to another rented home. Another retired man and I volunteered. We hired a three-ton van and went to their home. The wife, my friend, and I carried everything out to the van while the clergyman husband watched. I even moved the large fridge with the help of his wife while he stood by.

What must be noted is that all of these Sudanese men saw themselves as Christians, attended church regularly, and believed what they were doing was pleasing to God. They told me regularly, "Men were supposed to lead and domestic work is women's work. This is what the Bible teaches. You Australian Christians have it all wrong."

And to Conclude

I for one cannot believe God is pleased to see women regarded as second-class citizens, marginalized and so often abused in many ways in many parts of the world. And I cannot believe God is pleased to see men acting to further their own interests and being disrespectful and cruel to women, especially the one they have promised to love like Christ loved the church and which he gave his life for. To be quite specific, returning to Ron Sider's list, I cannot believe God is pleased to see female fetuses in the millions aborted, girls excluded from education, women underpaid for their work and going hungry, suffering for lack of medical care, physically abused and in danger of being sold into prostitution. If this is the result of believing that men should have precedence and that women are to be submissive, then I conclude we should reexamine our beliefs. We must be reading the Bible wrongly. Headship teaching, certainly in the developing world, does not seem to be "good for women, good for children and good for families."[13]

13. Moore, "After Patriarchy, What?," 576.

Chapter 4

Rightly Hearing the Bible Today

TODAY, THE CHURCHES ARE agreed, domestic abuse and violence is sinful; it is far too common in society and in the church communities; programs to educate people on this scourge are needed, and when abused women look to a pastor/minster for support and counsel they should be believed and supported. Where there is disagreement in the churches is on what the Bible says about the man-woman relationship. As I have already pointed out, those who call themselves "complementarians" believe that the Bible clearly teaches that in creation before the fall God set the man over the woman and this is the God-given ideal for all time. They thus speak of male leadership and female submission. In diametrical opposition those who call themselves "evangelical egalitarians" believe that in creation God made man and woman in his image and likeness and he appointed them both to rule over his world, side by side. The subordination of women is entirely a consequence of the fall; it is a reflection of sin (Gen 3:16). This understanding of the male-female relationship, they argue, is reflected in the teaching and example of Jesus.

This protracted disagreement on what the Bible actually teaches on the man-woman relationship is not simply an academic debate, it has profound consequences, especially for women. Complementarian theology makes man "first," woman "second." It makes man the leader, woman the submissive follower. No matter how euphemistically the complementarian case is put it demeans women. Worst of all it makes them vulnerable to abuse and violence in their own home. Needy and controlling men in the churches and among the clergy hear this teaching and put it into practice in their marriages. They insist on making all the major decisions, controlling what happens in the home, and in all things expecting submission by the wife. If she is not submissive the husband gets angry and abusive, often quoting the Bible's teaching on male headship. When men believe they are rightfully

RIGHTLY HEARING THE BIBLE TODAY

in charge, whether they are Christians or not, we know this is the context where abuse and violence in the home is most likely to occur.

What then does the Bible say on the man-woman relationship? This is not a question with a simple answer. No one can deny that in the Bible the world in which it is set is reflected. The biblical writers thought the sun revolved around the earth, the world was created in seven literal days, slavery and the whipping of slaves was normative, and women were subordinated to men. What we are seeking an answer on is, *what does the Bible make the God-given ideal for the man-woman relationship?* And what in the Bible speaks to our twenty-first-century historical and cultural context when none of the cultural assumptions of the biblical writers are taken for granted anymore?

Possible Consequences of Teaching that Men Are to Lead and Women Be Submissive

In churches with a complementarian pastor the congregation hear a lot about male headship. I have been told innumerable times, usually by despairing churchgoers, "Our pastor must mention headship teaching almost every week and he preaches on Ephesians 5:22–24 two or three times a year." I have taken several hundred weddings in a lifetime as a pastor. Next to 1 Corinthians chapter 13 on love, the most requested text to be read and preached on was Ephesians 5:22–24. Anxious young men marrying able young women invariably chose this text. But it is also by far the *most-quoted* text by abusers. Before we turn to this text let me tell you a true story.

In one of the churches where I was the minister/pastor, a couple in their early thirties started attending with their three-year old daughter. He was a lawyer, she a nurse. He had a very good knowledge of the Bible, thanks to his university days when he had belonged to the Christian Union. He was always very affable at morning tea and I thought they were happily married. Then one night the front door bell rang at about 8 p.m. There was "Julie" at the door with her little girl; they were both crying and obviously distressed. She asked to come in. I sat her down and Lynley joined us. She said that she and "Bruce" had had an awful row and he had slapped her across the face. She added,

> This is not the first time he has been violent. For the first six months of our marriage, "Bruce" was the most loving man I had ever met. He almost consumed me. Then slowly I began to feel overwhelmed by him and his demands. He wanted to know where

> I was going, what money I was spending, who I was seeing, and he seemed always to be angry. I became fearful of him . . . . After our evening meal tonight, he completely lost it and when I told him what he was saying was absurd he gave me a hard slap in the face.

Then I heard loud knocking on our front door. I left "Julie" with Lynley and went to the door. I opened it a little and quickly locked the security screen door. Standing before me was "Bruce," obviously very agitated. He asked, "Is 'Julie' here?" I said, "Yes." He asked to come in. I refused. He then said,

> You are a minister. The Bible says the husband is the head of his wife and she should obey him. "Julie" needs to come home. Don't believe what she tells you.

> When I continued to refuse him entry, he got more and more angry and agitated. He repeatedly quoted headship teaching to me. I eventually told him if he did not leave, I would call the police. I said, "Julie will not be coming home with you tonight."

I can remember that encounter with him as vividly as if it were yesterday.

This is not an exceptional story. Everyone who has had experiences with churchgoing wife abusers knows that they frequently quote the Bible, especially what Paul says on headship and wifely submission. They think the Bible puts them in charge and their wife should obey them. They are being what God wants them to be, a strong man in control. I have already quoted Ruth Tucker's account of what happened in her marriage and I repeat this story because it is so telling. For nineteen years she endured all manner of abuse: verbal, emotional, spiritual, sexual, and physical, from her evangelical pastor husband. The spiritual abuse involved his constant appeal to the Bible. He insisted that the Bible clearly taught that he was the head of the home and she should obey him. She says,

> During his violent rages, my ex-husband often hurled biblical texts at me, as though the principal tenet of Scripture was, "Wives, submit to your husbands." He spat the words out repeatedly, beating me over the head, at least figuratively, with his black-and-white Bible. His hitting and punching and slamming me, however, were anything but figurative. Nor were his terror-loaded threats. I felt trapped and feared for my life, while outwardly disguising bruises with long sleeves and clever excuses, pretending ours was a happy marriage.[1]

---

1. Tucker, *Black and White Bible*, 14.

Complementarians say often and loudly that nothing in the Bible encourages men to be abusive of their wives, or legitimates such behavior, but everyone who has been involved in domestic abuse in churchgoing families, or read about it, knows that Paul's words, "wives be subject to your husbands . . . for the husband is the head of the wife" (Eph 5:22–23), are invariably quoted by abusive churchgoing husbands in support of their behavior, and to justify it. This is something that cannot be denied. It also cannot be denied that complementarians teach that the man should be the leader in the home and the church, and women should be submissive. This means that in the church men should be pastors, not women, and in the home the husband should make all the important decisions (or "have the final casting vote").

In the face of the fact, now undeniable, that this headship teaching can encourage *some* Christian men to abuse and be violent to their wives, and in their minds justify this behavior, complementarians have to make the very hard choice for them to either go on dogmatically holding to their male headship doctrine or abandon it. They have to ask, if they have been wrong to ignore, categorically reject, and castigate evangelical egalitarians who for forty years have been loudly saying to them, "You are wrong. The Bible does not make the headship of men and the submission of women, the creation ideal. It reflects the fall and is not pleasing to God." Because Ephesians 5:21–33 is the only text in the Bible that speaks of the husband as the head of his wife it must get the most attention. What in fact does this passage teach?

Ephesians 5: 22–24: "The husband is the head of the wife."

In these verses, Paul undeniably speaks of the cultural reality of his day; the husband is the *kephalē*/head of his wife, and the wife should be subordinate/submissive *in all things* (v. 24). The Greek noun *kephalē*, in its literal sense, refers to the flesh-covered cranium, the top part of the body. It is thus a natural metaphor for the top part of something, what is uppermost, most prominent, preeminent.[2] "Head-over," and "source" are possible secondary metaphorical meanings of this word.[3] But however translated, the word *in this context* must imply preeminence in some sense

2. Cervin, "On the Significance of *Kephalē* (Head)"; Thiselton, *First Epistle to the Corinthians*, 812, 815, 817.

3. Thiselton, *First Epistle to the Corinthians*, 812–20.

because the wife is exhorted to be submissive/subordinate to the one who is her head. You are rightly submissive to those set over you. In hearing what Paul says in this verse, his first-century readers would not have blinked. Men had precedence in Judaism and the Greco-Roman world and this was never questioned. Paul's original readers must have "heard" Paul to be saying, the husband is the top part in the relationship; he is preeminent; therefore, you wives be subordinate.

There is, nevertheless, a profound question that must be asked, the same question that has to be asked when we hear Paul say to slaves, "obey your masters with fear and trembling . . . as you obey Christ" (Eph 6:5). Is Paul simply giving good practical advice to wives and slaves living in the first century where the subordination of women and slavery were taken-for-granted realities and never questioned, or in both cases prescribing how God has ordered the world for all time? This is a question no complementarian wants to consider. I have been angrily told many times, "If Paul says the man is the leader and the wife should submit to him, that settles it for me." It is, however, not quite so simple for me. One hundred and fifty years ago the best of evangelical and Reformed theologians in the Old South read Paul to be endorsing the institution of slavery, but today no Christian does this. We all believe slavery is an evil, a reflection of the fall. We all therefore argue that Paul's instruction to masters and slaves was good practical advice in the first century that is not applicable in any way in our age and culture. We agree slavery is an evil.

In seeking to exegete and apply rightly today what Paul says in Eph 5:22–24 on the leadership of the husband and the submission/subordination of the wife, three things must be noted and stressed:

1. Paul is not giving distinctive Christian teaching. Until modern times, and in most of the world today, men believe they should be in charge and women subordinate and obedient. All the great religions of the world teach just this, and the more fundamentalist they are the more they insist on this. There is nothing distinctively Christian or counter-cultural in Eph 5:22–24.

2. Paul does not ground what he says to wives and husbands in God's good creation before the fall. He makes no appeal to any part of Scripture for what he says in Eph 5:22–24. If he had appealed to Scripture, only one text would have given theological support, Gen 3:16. In this verse, as a consequence of her sin, God says to Eve, "Your husband will

rule over you." (Adam is also punished for his disobedience.) True, in v. 31 Paul quotes Gen 2:24, but not to ground women's subordination in the good creation before the fall. Rather, he quotes this text to speak of the oneness of the husband and wife in God's good creation order. This mysterious oneness, it is to be carefully noted, runs counter to the thought that God has set husbands over wives.

3. What Paul says immediately before, namely be subordinate to one another (v. 21) and what he says immediately after, "husbands, love your wives, just as Christ loved the church and gave himself up for her" (in death), and "husbands love your wife as you love your own body" (v. 28), completely subverts any thought that the husband rules over his wife and she like a slave should stand under his authority and obey him.[4] This is distinctively Christian and countercultural teaching.

Ephesians 5:22–24 in Context

One of the most basic rules for the right interpretation of any text or passage in Scripture is that the context must be considered. Nowhere is this truer than with Ephesians 5:22–24. If these verses are taken in isolation and read as an absolute timeless directive on the marriage relationship, the man should be in charge, he should make all the major decisions, and his wife should be submissive "in all things." We simply have proof-texting. *We are reading one text in isolation from its context and not taking into account what is said elsewhere in Scripture.* When the literary, historical, and the whole of the biblical contexts for any text are ignored, then the maxim is true, "a text without a context is a pretext for a proof text." Three contexts must be considered.

1. The Literary Context

First, we consider the literary context in which Eph 5:22–24 is set, considering both the wider context and the immediate context. In Ephesians chapter 5, Paul begins by exhorting Christians to live "a life of love" (5: 1); to shun sexual immorality (5:2–7); not to walk in darkness (5:8–14), but rather "be

---

4. The Greek word *hypotassō*, meaning "to stand under, be subordinate," implies obedience. Subordinates are to obey those set over them. Peter makes this explicit in 1 Pet 3:6.

filled with the Spirit" (5:12–20). Then he addresses specifically wives and husbands (5:21–33), parents and their children (of all ages) (6:1–4), and slaves and masters (6:5–9). Eph 5:21—6:9 is a literary unit, with 5:1–20 as an introduction. It is the longest of the so-called "household rules" given by the apostles (see also Col 2:18—4:1; 1 Pet 2:18—3:7).

In these rules for living in the extended family of the Greco-Roman world, the apostles tell Christians to accept the cultural social norms of their day and yet in each case Paul says something to subvert them in the light of the Christian ethic. This is firstly and most importantly seen in Eph 5:21 where Paul begins what he is about to say to the two parties in three paired relationships, "Be subject to one another out of reverence for Christ" (v. 21). In speaking of marriage, this subversive theme appears again when Paul commands husbands to love their wife like Christ loved the church and gave himself for her (Eph 5:25); in words to children and fathers it appears (in a whisper) when Paul tells fathers do not "exasperate" your children (Eph 6:4), and in the master-slave relationship, when he tells masters to remember Jesus Christ is their master as he is the master of their slave(s) (Eph 6:9).

The fact that these three paired exhortations in their literary context are given sequentially indicates they are of the same nature. To separate off the exhortation to husbands and wives, arguing this exhortation is timeless authoritative teaching because it is based on the "order of creation," while the exhortation to parents and children, and to masters and slaves, are simply practical, time-bound advice no longer binding in our historical context is special pleading. Paul nowhere mentions or alludes to a supposed hierarchical, pre-fall *creation order* where the husband rules over his wife, not in Eph 5:21–33, or anywhere else in his writings.[5] Let me say it emphatically, in Eph 5:22–24, Paul speaks of the taken-for-granted cultural reality: men rule over their wives, wives submit. Paul is tacitly accepting *the fallen order* where men rule over their wives, and asking Christian women in the first century to accept this reality. This fallen order is also reflected in slavery. God is not pleased to see those made in his image and likeness subjected by force and degraded, yet Paul (and Peter) accept that some will be masters and some slaves, and Paul starkly tells slaves to obey "your earthly masters . . . as you obey Christ" (Eph 6:5; cf. 1 Pet 2:18–25). If we do *not* take these

---

5. Not even in 1 Tim 2:13–14. See Giles, *What the Bible Actually Teaches*, 125–28. In this Timothy text, Paul illustrates from the Genesis story why he has forbidden certain women from teaching in a dictatorial way. Remember, he says to them, you were created second, and it was Eve who was first "deceived."

exhortations to slaves to be subordinate,[6] and to obey their masters, to be a reflection of God's perfect will, then we should not interpret apostolic exhortations to wives to be subordinate as a reflection of God's perfect will. In both cases, we rightly read these parallel exhortations as good practical advice to Christians, living in a culture where the subordination of wives and slavery were taken-for-granted realities.

If Paul is addressing children and teenagers in Eph 6:1–4, then this exhortation is not time-bound in some way, but this is almost certainly not the case. In the ancient world, offspring were obligated to their parents for all of their life.[7] This is not so today.

Now we note *the immediate literary context* of verses 22–24. Immediately preceding these words, Paul first of all says to husbands and wives, "Be subject to one another."[8] This is distinctive Christian teaching. Pope John-Paul II says this idea is radically counter cultural; it is "an innovation of the Gospel."[9] No one prior to Paul, the Pope says, had ever suggested that in a marriage, "subjection is not one sided but mutual."[10]

What follows after verses 22–24 is even more startling and revolutionary, given the first-century setting of Paul's epistles. Speaking specifically to Christian husbands in verses 25–31, Paul asks them to behave towards their wives in ways that starkly run counter to the cultural norm. He asks them to love their wives "just as Christ loved the church and gave himself for her" (v. 25) and to love them "as they love their own bodies" (v. 28). He does not use the Greek word *eros* (sexual love), or *philia* (brotherly/family love), but *agapē* (self-giving love), which as far as we know, no one before Paul had used for the marriage relationship. *Agapē* is the noblest and loftiest word in the Greek language for love. We understand its meaning through the self-sacrifice of Christ who "loved (*agapaō*) the church and gave himself up for her" (v. 25). Paul in 1 Corinthians 13 describes what this love involves. This kind of love is not an emotion, but a way of behaving. This is how Christian husbands are to give themselves for their wives. No one, save Christ, had ever suggested

6. 1 Pet 2:18; Titus 2:9.

7. The Greek word *teknon* refers to the offspring of a couple of any age. In the Greco-Roman world of the first century, a male or female *teknon* was under the authority of their father before they married and usually sons, when they married, continued to live under their father's authority under the one roof in the extended family.

8. Below I reply to those who claim in this one instance the reciprocal pronoun *allelōn*/one another, does not have reciprocal force.

9. John-Paul II, *Mulierus Dignitatem*, 88.

10. John-Paul II, *Mulierus Dignitatem*, 88.

anything like this. Here we have teaching, I say again, that is countercultural, radically new, and distinctively Christian.

Where Paul's emphasis lies should be carefully noted. In Eph 5:22–24, the apostle uses just forty-seven words to ask first-century Christian wives to accept their culturally prescribed lowly status. He uses 143 words to ask Christian husbands to act counterculturally and love their wives like Christ loved the church and gave his life for her. He only asks women to accept what they cannot change; he asks Christian men to change their whole way of behaving and thinking about their relationship with their wives. When modern-day complementarian preachers give most emphasis and most time to what Paul says in Eph 5:22–24, namely that the man is to be the head/leader and the wife be submissive *in all things*, they give the very opposite emphasis to Paul. His emphasis is on what is new and distinctively Christian, namely marital mutual subordination and the husband loving his wife to the point of giving his life for her and serving her.

Let me reiterate clearly what I have just said. In Ephesians 5:21 and 25–32 we find teaching on marriage that is historically sharply countercultural, revolutionary, *and distinctively Christian*. It is "an innovation of the Gospel."[11] In these verses, Paul introduces the Christian understanding of leadership prescribed by Jesus and applies it to husbands. A leader is one who serves, even to the point of giving one's life for another.

In reply, complementarians say in Eph 5:25–33 Paul is simply telling Christian husbands that they are "head-over" their wives, adding that this supposedly God-given authority over their wives should be exercised in a loving and servant-like way. No, Paul is asking Christian husbands to lay aside their power, authority, preeminence, and privileges given to them as part of this fallen world (Gen 3:16) and instead love and serve their wives even to the point of giving their life for them. This is "headship" turned on its head.

2. The Historical Context

Paul wrote Eph 5:22–24 in the first-century Greco-Roman world where the rule of the husband and the subordination of the wife; the right of men to own slaves and the need for slaves to obey their masters were taken-for-granted realities, not challenged by Paul or anyone else at that time. In this world the vast majority of women, who were not educated except in home

11. John-Paul II, *Mulierus Dignitatem*, 88.

duties, once married were either pregnant or nursing children for most of their life, and in an urban setting were expected to stay within the home. They could not support themselves financially. They were dependent on and set under a man for all of their life: father, husband, guardian. In this cultural context, subordination was the lot of children, slaves, and women. Free men were supposed to be assertive, in control, and to manage. They were to look after their own interests. Husbands had rights, privileges, and freedoms denied to wives, and they held most of the power, and provided all the income, even if they conveniently left the management of the home to their wives (1 Tim 5:14). It is in this historical context Paul says to wives and slaves, accept your lot in life. To hear Scripture rightly in the twenty-first century, we cannot ignore that what he said in Eph 5:22–24 was given in a first-century historical and cultural context.

3. The Whole of the Bible Context

My most formative theological teacher, Dr. Broughton Knox, the principal of Moore Theological College in my days as a student, used to say regularly, "the most important context to interpret any one verse or passage in the Bible is the whole Bible." His pithy maxim reflects the principle that no one text or passage in Scripture should be read to contradict what is clearly taught elsewhere in Scripture. Looking at the big picture on what the Bible says on marriage, what do we learn?

1. The term "headship" does not appear at all in the Bible.

2. Writing to Timothy, Paul says married women "are to manage (Greek *despotēs*, rule) their home"—they are in other words, to be "the head of the home" (1 Tim 5:14). In the Greco-Roman world, the wife was in charge of all domestic matters; the man's domain was the public arena.[12]

3. There are only two instances in the whole Bible where the Greek word *kephalē*, translated *into* English as "head," is used in connection with the male-female relationship (1 Cor 11:3; Eph 5:23), and in the first instance the wife-husband relationship is not in view. Whatever Paul implies is the metaphorical meaning of this Greek word in each context,

---

12. On this matter see further Giles, *What the Bible Actually Teaches*, 108–9.

what is clear is that the idea that the husband is the *kephalē*/head of his wife is not a major theme in Paul's epistles. He mentions it just once.

4. In God's good creation, before the fall, God unambiguously gives the same status, dignity, and leadership potential to man and woman (Gen 1:27–28), and explicitly makes the rule of the man over the woman entirely a consequence of the fall (Gen 3:16), an expression of sin.

5. In the Gospels, Jesus says not one word on male headship/leadership, or wifely submission, and much to the contrary.[13] What is more, for Jesus, leadership in his community, he says seven times, is not about power/ authority over others, but about humble, self-giving service for others; the laying aside of all thought of ruling over others (Matt 20:26–28; 23:11; Mark 9:35; 10:43–45; Luke 9:48; 22:24–27; John 13:4–20).

6. In Paul's longest discussion on marriage in 1 Cor 7:1–40 he envisages a Christian marriage to be a fully equal and reciprocal relationship with mutual responsibilities.[14] He gives no precedence to the husband.

7. In Col 3:18–19 we find a brief summary of what Paul says to husbands and wives in Eph 5:21–33 but we find no exhortation to mutual sub-ordination, or any mention of the idea that "the husband is the head of the wife." Paul reiterates his exhortation to husbands, "love your wives," adding "never treat them harshly" (Col 3:19)—which may be taken to mean positively, if you love your wife you will treat her re-spectfully and gently.

What this means is that most of what the Bible says on the marriage rela-tionship gives no support to the idea that God wills that the man should rule over his wife and the wife should submit; indeed it seems to exclude the thought that this is God's good and perfect will, binding until the end of all things. Genesis 3:16 certainly says the man will rule over his wife, but all agree this text speaks of what is not good; of marriage not according God's good and perfect will.

---

13. On the significance of the historical fact that the twelve apostles were all men, see Giles, *What the Bible Actually Teaches*, 87–89. What seems to be most important is that they were twelve in number not men. This symbolized that they were the new Israel.

14. See my extended discussion on 1 Corinthians chapter 7 in Giles, *What the Bible Actually Teaches*, 169–71.

Two Contrasting Understandings of Marriage

What is now clear is that in Eph 5:21–33 we have two contrasting and irreconcilable understandings of marriage standing side by side, a radically new and distinctively Christian one, and one that is as old as the fall and which prevails in this world. This argument is very hard for most evangelicals to accept. They fear it might undermine their high view of Scripture. My high view of Scripture demands I accept what I find in Scripture.

In support of my argument that in Eph 5:21–33 we find two contrasting and irreconcilable understandings of marriage, I note that both evangelical egalitarians and complementarians do hermeneutical gymnastics to get around this problem. They seek ways to minimize any possible tension in what Paul says.

Evangelical egalitarians often argue that *kephalē*/head in this passage does not imply the idea "head-over"/ "authority over," but rather "source." This is a possibility; the Greek word can definitely carry this meaning, but this does not overcome the tension. Paul goes on to ask wives specifically to be subordinate. We are rightly subordinate to those set over us.

Complementarians seek to overcome this stark tension between what is said on the one hand in vv. 22–24, and on the other, in vv. 21 and 25–33, by explaining away anything that would undermine the idea that the husband rules over the wife. They do this in two ways. First, they argue that the exhortation to be subordinate to one another (v. 21) is not reciprocal in any strict way. The argument is as follows:[15]

1. Wherever the word *hypotassō*/submit is found in the New Testament it implies an ordered relationship where one party is set over another.

2. The reciprocal pronoun, *allelōn*/one another, does not always indicate the same action by both parties.

3. Paul cannot be asking for mutual subordination because wives are to submit to their husbands, not husbands to wives.

None of these arguments have any force whatsoever.

1. Paul some thirty times calls on Christians to exercise a "one another ministry."[16] In most cases, what is asked is characteristically the

---

15. It is most fully set out in O'Brien, *Letter to the Ephesians*, 399–404. See also Köstenberger and Köstenberger, *God's Design*, 182–84; Grudem, "Myth of Mutual Submission."

16. I give all the references in Giles, *Patterns of Ministry*, 39.

prerogative of one party, serving, teaching, forgiving, caring, etc., yet the apostle makes it reciprocal. To ask for mutual subordination is perfectly in line with many other *one another* exhortations. Indeed, on a personal level, I find no problems with this exhortation. My wife and I try to subordinate ourselves to each other every day.

2. In every example where Paul uses the reciprocal pronoun, *allelōn*/one another, it has reciprocal force as we would expect with a reciprocal pronoun![17] The examples given by complementarians, supposedly where this is not the case, are completely unconvincing.[18]

3. The argument that Paul could not be asking for mutual subordination because he then goes on to ask wives only to be subordinate, is to say what Paul can ask and what he cannot ask.

Possibly, the most telling weakness of this distinctively complementarian argument that the reciprocal pronoun, *allelōn*/one another, is not reciprocal in this one instance is that a significant number of leading complementarians reject it, arguing it is special pleading,[19] which it is.

The second way complementarian theologians seek to get around the stark tension between what is said on the one hand in vv. 21 and 25–33 and in vv. 22–24 on the other hand is to argue that the man's headship/authority over his wife is to be exercised in a loving and servant-like way. In this argument they draw on the English idiom that speaks of kings, rulers, policemen, and other authority figures "serving." Authority figures may exercise their power humbly, conscientiously, and well but they do not in fact serve—behave like servants. They rule; they command and others obey. Servants in contrast serve; they do as they are told.

Jesus recognized this fact with great clarity and force. Some seven times he set in stark juxtaposition how the powerful in this world lead and how his disciples are to lead (Matt 20:26–28; 23:11; Mark 9:35; 10:43–45; Luke 9:48; 22:24–27; John 13:4–20). The powerful of this world lead by "lording it over" others (Luke 22:24). They command, others obey. To his disciples, Jesus says, "It shall not be so among you." You are to be servants;

---

17. Payne, *Man and Woman*, 279.

18. I examine these and find none of them convincing in Giles, *What the Bible Actually Teaches*, 159–60.

19. For example, Knight, "Husbands and Wives as Analogues,"167–68; and Arnold, *Ephesians*, 356. For telling evangelical egalitarian replies to this argument, see Payne, *Man and Woman*, 279–81; Marshall, "Mutual Love and Submission," 195–98.

you are to give yourself in lowly service. In John 13 we are told how Jesus illustrated what is involved in being a servant. He took a towel, kneeled, and washed the dirty feet of his disciples. In Eph 5:25–31 Paul asks Christian husbands to lay aside their power and privileges given to them as part of this fallen world (Gen 3:16) and instead love and serve their wives even to the point of giving their life for them. This is "headship" turned on its head. We see just how deaf complementarians are to what Paul is actually saying when complementarian warriors the Köstenbergers say, "servant leadership is biblical, but not leadership drained of all notions of authority."[20] And, they add, Christian servant leaders "have real authority to which others are called to submit."[21]

Once we recognize that in Eph 5:22–24 Paul is speaking specifically of *the fallen ordering of this world,* we see how countercultural and revolutionary is what he says before in v. 21 and after in vv. 25–33.

Let me in brief reiterate what I have argued. *Ephesians 5:22–24 does not tell us "what the Bible clearly teaches about the marriage relationship"—it does not give the God-given model of marriage. It tells us rather how marriages in Paul's day operated, and often do today. The distinctive Christian understanding of marriage is given in Ephesians 5:21 and 5:25–33.*

1 Pet 3:1–6

Another passage of huge importance in discussing domestic abuse is 1 Pet 3:1–6. Many complementarians appeal to this text to make the point that the submission/subordination of the wife implies obedience (1 Pet 3:6) and that abuse and violence in a marriage are not a valid reason for a wife to divorce her husband.

In addressing wives, Peter begins, "Wives in the same way." By using the conjunction *homoiōs,* meaning "likewise or in the same way,"[22] Peter parallels what he has just said to slaves. What exactly he parallels is not made explicit; likewise, be submissive, *or,* likewise be submissive even if your husband is harsh and cruel. Before 1960 most commentators, and today many complementarians, take *homoiōs*/likewise/in the same way to be saying, like slaves, you wives are to be subordinate/submissive and accept your suffering even if your husband is harsh and cruel. Thus for

20. Köstenberger and Köstenberger, *God's Design,* 186.

21. Köstenberger and Köstenberger, *God's Design,* 189.

22. This Greek word means "in a similar way."

example, Wayne Grudem says, Peter uses *homoiōs*/likewise to indicate that wives like slaves should be subordinate to their husbands "in motive (for the Lord's sake (2:13), in extent of application (to good or harsh masters [2:18] or husbands [3:1]), and in attitude (with proper respect, 2:18; 3:2), as well as in the main concept of submission to authority (2:18; 3:1)."[23] I suspect many first-century Christian women on hearing Peter's words would have taken his "likewise" in this sense, even if the apostle did not make this connection explicit.

A number of speakers at the Sydney Diocesan Synod in 2018 took the "likewise" in this way, arguing that 1 Pet 3:1–6 excluded domestic abuse and violence as valid basis for divorce and remarriage. On turning to "Dr. Google," with one click I found a sermon by Pastor Stephen J. Cole, a well-known complementarian, making this point in a sermon:

> Peter's words, "even if any of them are disobedient to the word" show that he wasn't just thinking about nice husbands. So, we must conclude that a wife may need to submit to some abuse. The difficult question is, How much? My view is that a wife must submit to verbal and emotional abuse, but if the husband begins to harm her physically, she needs to call civil or church authorities. There are civil laws against battery and it is proper for an abused wife to call in authorities to confront and deal with a husband who violates the law. Although physical abuse is not a biblical basis for divorce, I would counsel separation in some cases to protect the wife while the husband gets his temper under control. But even in such situations, a Christian wife must not provoke her husband to anger and she must display a gentle spirit.[24]

Pastor Cole is unambiguous, "physical abuse is not a biblical basis for divorce," and a wife should submit to her husband no matter what he does.

In our new cultural context where good marriages are profoundly equal, the abuse of one's wife is totally unacceptable, and a crime punishable by the state, and women are not expected to be submissive and obedient to their husbands, we must ask, is Peter prescribing how Christians should live in the twenty-first century? Again, we study the text in the light of its literary, historical, and biblical contexts.

---

23. Grudem, "Wives Like Sarah," 201.
24. Cole, "Living with a Difficult Husband."

1. The Literary Context

The epistle of 1 Peter addresses Christians who are suffering for their faith, and slaves and wives are singled out as examples of those suffering. 1 Pet 3:1–6 stands in the middle of a section beginning at 2:11 and ending at 3:22. Peter begins with a general exhortation to believers, "conduct yourself honorably among Gentiles" (unbelievers). He then moves to three particular examples of what this will involve, in each case linked by the command to submit (*hypotassō*) (2:13; 2:18; 3:1). First, he says Christians should submit to those set over them, and he mentions the emperor and local governors (2:13–17). Second, he says, Christian slaves should submit to their masters who are almost certainly Christians,[25] whether they be kind or harsh. Even if their master beats them, Peter says, they should accept this and not complain. In behaving in this way, he adds, they are following the example of Jesus. Third, he tells wives to be submit to and "obey" their husband (1 Peter 3:6). Peter's words to slaves and wives are given sequentially and cannot be separated, let alone contrasted. His use of the conjunction *homoiōs*/likewise/ in the same way in 2:1 makes this explicit.

2. The Historical Context

Peter is writing to first-century Christians in the Roman Empire who knew nothing about democracy; slavery and the beating of slaves were normative, and wives were set under the authority of their husbands and were often beaten.[26] The apostles' exhortations to citizens, slaves, and wives made perfect sense in the first century AD but they cannot be consistently and honestly applied today. In our democratically governed, modern-day context, we should at times question or oppose our rulers; we should absolutely reject slavery and see it as sinful, and by inference the beating of workers; make the fully equal marriage our ideal, and abhor abuse and violence in

25. The evidence for this assertion is: 1. In the Roman empire the religion of the master was almost invariably the religion of the slave. 2. Since Paul exhorts masters he must be speaking to Christian masters. 3. Christians owned slaves in the early church. Philemon was a Christian slave owner.

26. I sometimes see in complementarian literature the claim that it was illegal to beat one's wife in the Roman Empire. There were laws protecting women with Roman citizenship but these were not enforced and Peter is not addressing Roman citizens. On the practice of wife beating in the first century see the well-documented discussion in Reeder, "1 Peter 3:1–6."

any marriage. To assert that Peter's words to wives apply today and the other two directives do not is special pleading. There is nothing in the text to suggest this, and as Peter deals with these matters sequentially it seems very unlikely. Again, we find no appeal to a supposed creation order in which men are set over women. Peter's exhortation to wives to be subordinate is entirely evangelistically motivated. He asks wives to accept their culturally prescribed subordinate status "so that" husbands who are not believers "may be won over without a word by their wives conduct."

Slaves in Peter's day had to endure abuse and violence. They could not leave their master. No law protected them. It was much the same for wives, they could not as a general rule leave their husbands no matter what he did to them. But in neither instance is this the case today. Slavery is illegal and judged to be immoral and the state does not condone any abuse or violence in the employer-employee relationship. Women workers' bodies are not owned by their employer. Slavery and working for a wage are to be contrasted not compared. Likewise, in the husband-wife relationship today, the state does not condone abuse or violence by a man in the home. He is liable to be charged for such behavior. What is more, a woman is free to leave her husband if he abuses her. As difficult as it may be for her to leave for many reasons, if she flees the state will protect her. We should not think that Peter was indifferent to the suffering and abuse of slaves, or that of some wives. He simply asks slaves and possibly wives to accept suffering and abuse because in his day there were no other options.

It is slaves and wives living in this first-century historical context that Peter addresses. Not workers or wives in the twenty-first century.

3. The Whole of Bible Context

In stark contrast to Eph 5:21–33, this text in its entirety reflects exactly the historical and cultural context in which it is located. There is nothing that introduces a counter-cultural, Christian vision of marriage where mutual subordination and self-giving love transform a Christian marriage. The word "love," in any of its Greek forms, is not even mentioned. Read in the light of the whole Bible, 1 Pet 3:1–6 cannot be taken to give the Christian vision of marriage. Nothing makes this plainer than the fact that the word "love" is not mentioned.

What we have in 1 Pet 2:11—3:22 is inspired Scripture addressing the first-century situation that is time-bound. It cannot and should not be applied to citizens, workers, or wives in the twenty-first century. To appeal to 1 Pet 3:1–6 in support of wifely submission and obedience, and to exclude abuse and violence in a marriage as a valid basis for a wife to divorce her husband, is just bad theology. When promulgated by evangelical theologians it is self-serving theology.

Preaching on 1 Peter 2:18–25

It is a sobering thought that 150 years ago, white evangelical and Reformed clergy in the Old South of America loved to preach on 1 Pet 2:18–25.[27] This was the most preached-on text. In these sermons the following points were usually made to the masters and the slaves in church:

1. Nothing in the Bible encourages slave owners to be cruel or violent to their slaves.

2. God has ordered this world, setting masters above slaves and for this reason slaves should accept their subordinate status.

3. Slavery is not an evil; God instituted it to "produce holiness and happiness" in slaves.[28]

4. Even if your master is harsh, you must accept this. It is not a valid reason for you as a slave to flee. Remember that Jesus unjustly endured suffering; suffering is not evil.

   > It is commendable if you bear up under the pain of unjust suffering because you are conscious of God. If you endure when you are beaten for doing wrong, what credit is that? But if you endure when you do right, and suffer for it, you have God's approval (1 Pet 2:20–21).

5. You slaves may need to suffer much in this world, but this is a small matter in the light of your reward in heaven. It is "only for a little while you have to suffer various trials" (1 Pet 1:6).

And they would have ended their sermon by saying, "This is what the Bible clearly teaches." If they were preaching through 1 Peter, they may well have

---

27. I have discussed slavery and the appeal to the Bible for support in a number of my publications. The longest discussion on this is in *Trinity and Subordinationism*, 215–58. On pro-slavery sermons specifically, see Dill, *Rhetorical Analysis of Selective Pro-Slavery Sermons*.

28. Noll, *Civil War*, 54. See also 2, 6, 47.

concluded by saying, "Next week we will consider what Peter says to wives in the section following that begins, 'Likewise wives.'"

This sermon could not be preached today. We are all agreed slavery is an evil that degrades human beings made in the image and likeness of God. It is not pleasing to God. It is sinful. What this means is that today we clearly recognize that these Southern preachers were using the Bible to maintain their privileges and power. They were endorsing what God abhors. We cannot sidestep this very difficult conclusion by arguing Peter's words to slaves are still applicable; they speak to the employer-employee relationship. I say again, ordinary work, no matter how demanding, is to be contrasted with rather than compared to slavery. The master owns the slave like one owns a dog or horse and he has absolute authority over him or her. The slave labors to avoid the whip, the worker labors for a reward, and women workers are not sexually available by custom or law to their boss.

If the exhortations to slaves in no way speak to modern life, how can complementarians, if they want to be consistent, honestly insist that Peter's parallel exhortation to wives to be submissive *and to obey* their husbands apply today? The only difference between these parallel exhortations standing in sequence is that the one to slaves is more firmly grounded in the example of Jesus' unjust suffering. In other words, it has stronger theological support.

In good conscience, I argue that this passage in our age and culture does not ask married women to be submissive and obedient simply because they are women and for no other reason, or suffer abuse and violence at the hand of their husbands, and it does not exclude a woman leaving a husband who degrades her by abuse and leaves her fearful of her own safety and possibly of her children as well.

1 Timothy 2:8–15

This text is not quoted as a general rule in discussions about domestic abuse and violence but I must briefly comment on it because this is the primary text that complementarians use to exclude women from church leadership and preaching. If they did not have this one text, they would have nothing to make their case against the ordination of women. In excluding women from church leadership and preaching complementarians imply that women are second grade church members. There are some things they cannot do simply because they are women, and for no other reason. God has put men first in the church; women second. This devaluing of women creates an environment where the abuse of women will flourish, as Southern Baptists and Sydney Anglicans have discovered.

Egalitarian evangelicals and complementarians give opposing interpretations of this text. For all complementarians what is said in this text is *normative* for all times; women are not to exercise authority or teach in church and this prohibition is grounded in the order of creation that can never change. For all egalitarian evangelicals, this text gives *exceptional* teaching speaking to a specific situation in the church in Ephesus in the first century, not applicable in other contexts. This prohibition is entirely context specific and not grounded in a supposed creation order that sets men over women.

The argument that 1 Tim 2:8–15 gives *exceptional* teaching is compelling. I give the evidence.[29]

1. Nowhere else in the Bible do we read of men praying in anger and disputation (1 Tim 2:8). These words imply a church where some men, possibly many, are very angry about something. Church members are obviously divided and at loggerheads. An exceptional and ugly situation is certainly implied.

2. Nowhere else are women singled out as alone needing to be instructed (1 Tim 2:11). That women *only* are exhorted to learn implies that women in particular in Ephesus were in need of sound teaching.

3. Nowhere else are women told to learn in "quietness"[30] and in "full submission" (1 Tim 2:11).[31] This submission is best taken as submission to the sound doctrine they are to learn. Because the husband-wife relationship never comes into view in this passage, this submission can hardly refer to the submission of wives to husbands.

4. Nowhere else are women forbidden to teach in church. Elsewhere, Paul speaks of a woman apostle (Rom 16:7), and apostles certainly taught; of women prophesying (1 Cor 11:5), and prophesying was

29. For a fuller discussion on this text see Giles, *Patterns of Ministry*, 195–216; and Giles, *What Does the Bible Actually Teach*, 118–29, 130–34, 144–51.

30. The Greek word *hesuchia* sometimes translated "silence" speaks rather of quietness, of listening attentively. See Payne, *Man and Woman*, 314–15.

31. Some see 1 Cor 14:33–34 as a parallel but this text is almost certainly not from the pen of Paul. It is a marginal gloss later copied into the letter either after v. 33 or after v. 40. See Payne, *Man and Woman*, 217–70 and Payne, "Vaticanus Distigme-Obelos."

certainly a form of preaching; and of women house church leaders (Col 4:15), who certainly must have had authority in their own home. Then we must note that Paul's theology of ministry spelt out in 1 Corinthians 12 to 14 is predicated on Spirit-gifting, not gender.

5. Nowhere else in the New Testament do we find the Greek word *authentein* (v. 12). The meaning of this word may be disputed but that the word is exceptional cannot be disputed. It almost certainly speaks of domineering or usurped authority.[32]

6. Nowhere else in the whole Bible is it suggested that the *chronological order* of the creation of the sexes given in Genesis 2 ("For Adam was formed first") is significant (1 Tim 2:13). This is definitely not suggested by Genesis 1–3. In Genesis 1 man and woman are created last and yet they stand supreme, and in Genesis 2 Adam is created after the earth and yet rules over it.

7. Nowhere else in the whole Bible are we told that Adam was "not deceived" (v. 14). In Rom 5:12–19 and 1 Cor 15:20–22, Paul makes Adam the chief sinner; the one responsible for sin in the world. Furthermore, if Paul is exonerating Adam from sin in 1 Timothy 2, then he would be at odds with Genesis 2–3 where Adam and Eve alike sin and alike are punished for their sin.

8. Nowhere else are we told that Eve's deception in the Garden by the Devil is a warning exclusively to women. In 2 Cor 11:3 Paul says Eve's deception by the Devil is a warning to all Christians, men and women.

   These two appeals to Genesis chapters 1–3 are illustrative of what had happened in Ephesus in the first century. Some women had usurped authority, putting themselves "first." Like Eve they had been "deceived." There is no appeal here to a supposed pre-fall subordination of women.

9. Nowhere else are we told that women will be "saved through bearing children" (1 Tim 2:15).[33] How to interpret this perplexing comment is much disputed but no one can identify anything at all like it anywhere else in Scripture. This last startling comment on its own cries

---

32. Giles, *What the Bible Actually Teaches*, 144–51.

33. I am not convinced that Paul is here teaching that women will be saved through bearing children, but on face value this is what he seems to say. Elsewhere Paul is quite emphatic, salvation is found through faith in Christ alone, not works.

out that something exceptional involving women lies behind all that is said in 1 Tim 2:8–15.

How anyone can think that 1 Tim 2:8–15 gives normative teaching applying to the church in all ages completely escapes me. Virtually everything said in this passage has no parallel in the Bible and several things said seem to directly contradict what is clearly taught elsewhere.

Then there is another problem. In the first century, Christians met in homes in relatively small numbers, where everyone was free to minister and teach (Rom 15:4; Eph 5:19; Col 3:16; cf. Eph 4:35; Col 3:1). There were no ordained leaders who were the pastors of the church and who did most of the preaching.[34] This is the historical reality lying behind 1 Tim 2:8–14. How, we must ask, can this first-century experience of church speak to the church of the twenty-first century? Today, Christians meet in special buildings, can have anything from 5 to a 5,000 present, and have ordained clergy with three or more years of theological training who do most of the work out front. Like with the texts asking slaves and wives to be subordinate/submissive, we cannot simply assume what is said by the apostles in the first century applies one for one in the twenty-first century as complementarians do. The fact is marriages today and church life today must be *contrasted, rather than compared* with marriages and church life then. Thus, how to rightly apply today what is said in 1 Tim 2:8–15 is not self-evident. In fact, it is hard to see how it does apply.

A Hermeneutical Failure

We are now are at a point where we see clearly where complementarians get things wrong. Rightly interpreting Scripture in its historical context and rightly applying it in its contemporary setting is the domain of the science and art called *hermeneutics*. For many complementarians, Andreas and Margaret Köstenberger's 2014 book, *God's Design for Men and Women*, is taken as the most scholarly and up-to-date exposition of the complementarian position. Eighteen of the best-known and most-able evangelicals give glowing endorsements of their book. Andreas tells us that one of his specialties is hermeneutics. He says he has recently co-authored a book on

---

34. All this reflects the scholarly consensus. For more on all this, see my book, *Patterns of Ministry Among the First Christians*.

this.[35] In *God's Design,* he says, the most basic and primary hermeneutical rule is to distinguish and keep separate the so-called "two horizons" of Scripture. The first "horizon" is the biblical text which must be interpreted in its own literary and historical context, strenuously avoiding imposing our modern-day theology, concerns, or beliefs (especially on gender relations) onto the text. The second "horizon" is the contemporary world. Here the goal is to make the right application in the present of what was said in the past. Keeping strictly to this rule, Andreas says, "safeguards the authority of scripture."[36] I agree 100 percent with everything he says. My problem is that I see Andreas and all complementarians blatantly breaching this very rule when it comes to texts that speak of married women and the church and ministry. They conflate the two horizons making what is said in the first horizon directly applicable in the second horizon, and not even recognizing that they are doing this.

Malachi 2:16a

Complementarians who argue that abuse and violence in a marriage is not a ground for divorce, as far as the Bible is concerned, love to quote Malachi 2:16a, to say, "I hate divorce, says the Lord" (RSV, NRSV, NASB), and interpret it to mean that all divorce, except the case of adultery (Matt 19:9) and desertion by an unbelieving partner (1 Cor 7:15), is not acceptable to God. This text was quoted by several speakers against the motion that abuse and violence were a ground for divorce and remarriage before the chair at the 2018 annual Sydney Diocesan Synod.[37]

There are many problems with such appeals to this text. In the RSV, NRSV, and NASB translations, the verse goes on to say, "and I hate covering one's garment with violence." In these translations we are told that God hates both divorce and violence in a marriage. Then we have the problem that the text cannot be taken to imply an absolute prohibition on divorce—God hates divorce in every instance—unless Moses is being contradicted (Deut 24:1–4). Many Old Testament texts allow divorce (Lev 22:13; Num 30:9; Deut 22:13–19; Ezek 10:5, 11).

---

35. Köstenberger and Köstenberger, *God's Design,* 321.

36. Köstenberger and Köstenberger, *God's Design,* 337.

37. Several people present told me this was the case, and Mark Thompson, on reading this section of my book did not object to this claim but said he personally did not appeal to 1 Pet 3:1–6.

But the insurmountable problem with taking Malachi to be saying "I hate divorce, says the Lord" is that the authoritative Hebrew has the verb in the third-person singular (he hates), not first-person singular (I hate). It is most likely that the "he" is the man who hates and divorces his wife and in doing so behaves unfaithfully.[38] This is how the *New International Version* 2011 (NIV) translates the Hebrew. "The man who hates and divorces his wife, says the LORD, the God of Israel, does violence to the one he should protect, says the LORD Almighty. So be on your guard, and do not be unfaithful." In this translation of the Hebrew, divorcing one's wife is described as an act of violence. The *English Standard Version* (ESV) renders the Hebrew, "For the man who does not love his wife but divorces her, says the LORD, the God of Israel, covers his garment with violence."

I think the only conclusion we can draw is that Mal 2:16 should not be quoted to forbid a woman leaving her abusive husband or divorcing him. Indeed, this text may be condemning men who abuse and are violent to their wives. David Instone Brewer in his definitive study, *Divorce and Remarriage in the Bible,* says what Malachi is saying is that God hates the "person who causes the divorce by not being faithful to the marriage covenant."[39] It is his view that, "Physical and emotional abuse are extreme failures of the marriage covenant."[40] Craig Keener in his book, *. . . And Marries Another: Divorce and Remarriage in the New Testament,* comes to a similar conclusion. He asks, "Can we honestly maintain that a valid marriage exists when one spouse is treated only as an object for venting the other's repressed, violent rage? Is this not infidelity in some sense?"[41]

God Hates Abuse

In any attempt to think biblically on any big question, what the Bible says as a whole is what is most important. There is much in the Bible that makes it clear by inference that for man to abuse or be violent to his wife displeases God; "God hates abuse." With very little work I find innumerable passages

---

38. Mowczko, "God on Divorce (Mal 2:16)". See also on this text, Roberts, *Not Under Bondage,* 127–31.

39. Instone Brewer, *Divorce and Remarriage in the Bible,* 106.

40. Instone Brewer, *Divorce and Remarriage in the Bible,* 308.

41. Keener, *. . . And Marries Another,* 106.

in Scripture that make the abuse of or violence towards one's wife contrary to Scripture.[42]

- The Bible says: God condemns those who oppress the weak and vulnerable, especially women and children (Prov 14:31; Isa 1:15–17; Jer 22:3, 17; Ezek 22:7, 27–29; Mic 6:12; Matt 23:14; Mark 12:40; etc.).

- The Bible says: God will "cut off" those who are violent and abusive (Jud 19:5; Ps 11:5, 140:11; Prov 6:17; Jer 7:6; 22:3; Ezek 7:11; 8:17; Amos 3:10; Mic 6:8–12; and probably Mal 2:17; etc.).

- The Bible says: the leaders of God's people should protect and support the vulnerable and the weak (Ps 10:1–18; Prov 24:11–12; Isa 1:17; 3:14–25; Jer 22:3, 13–19; Zech 7:10; Jas 5:2–6; etc.).

- The Bible makes "the Golden Rule," the "gold standard" for all Christian behavior, "Do to others as you would have them do to you" (Matt 7:12). (This rule is broken by every abusive husband.)

- The Bible tells us that Jesus taught that to be angry with another may well lead to hell (Matt 5:21–26). And he said that a good person speaks good words, an evil person evil words, and adds, "by your words you will be condemned" (Matt 12:33–36). He also said it is what comes out of our mouth that defiles us (Matt 15:18–20). James on his part says, "You must understand this, my beloved: let everyone be quick to listen, slow to speak, slow to anger; for your anger does not produce God's righteousness" (Jas 1:19–20). "If anyone thinks they are religious, and they do not bridle their tongues . . . their religion is worthless" (Jas 1:26). With God's help they must tame their tongue because, "the tongue is a fire" (Jas 3:1–12). Paul puts the point positively, "Let no evil talk come out of your mouth, but only what is useful for building up, as there is need, so that your words may give grace to those who hear" (Eph 4:29).

- Paul says: "Love is patient; love is kind; love is not envious or boastful or arrogant or rude. *It does not insist on its own way*; it is not irritable or resentful" (1 Cor 13:4–5).

- Paul says to husbands: "love your wives, and never treat them harshly" (Col 3:19); "love your wives, just as Christ loved the church and gave himself up for her" (Eph 5:25), love your wife as you do your own body . . . "for no one even hates his own body, but he nourishes and

42. For more passages see "100 Verses on Domestic Abuse and Violence."

tenderly cares for it" (Eph 5:28–29). Peter on his part says, "Husbands show consideration for your wives in your life together, paying honor to the woman as the weaker partner" (1 Pet 3:7).

Finally

In conclusion, I say to my complementarian friends yet again, please consider afresh what the Bible actually teaches on women and how it applies in the twenty-first century. The overall biblical picture places man and woman side by side with heads erect. Teaching that men are to lead and women be submissive as the creation ideal that can never change devalues women and all too often leads to their abuse.

You must go back to Scripture because,

> The latest international evidence shows that there are certain factors that consistently predict—or drive—higher levels of violence against women. These include beliefs and behaviors reflecting disrespect for women, low support for gender equality and an adherence to or rigid or stereotyped gender roles, relations and identities.[43]

---

43. "Change the Story," Foreword, 1.

Chapter 5

Conclusion

ABOUT A HUNDRED AND fifty years ago, the wide ranging and seemingly watertight "biblical case" for slavery, developed by the best of Reformed theologians in the Old South of the United States, began to be called into question, not by counter biblical arguments, which they dismissed categorically, but by appeals to books which described what slavery actually involved for the enslaved—constant abuse and violence.[1] This was an extremely difficult development for the pro-slavery evangelical theologians because they had consistently and strongly argued for years that slavery was a "benevolent" institution, "a positive good."[2] It "produces holiness and happiness" in the slaves.[3] The most significant accounts describing what slavery was actually like for Africans in America were John Newton's 1787 book, *Thoughts on the African Slave Trade;* Theodore Weldt's 1839 book, *American Slavery As It Is: Testimony of a Thousand Witnesses,* and Harriet Beecher Stowe's *Uncle Tom's Cabin: Life Among the Lowly,* published in 1852, which became the best-selling novel of the nineteenth century. These books convinced many people that there must be something wrong with the "biblical" case for slavery, despite the many texts quoted in support of it, and the repeated claims that it was "good" for slaves. A "theology" that led to the devaluing of those made in the image and likeness of God, extensive cruelty and abuse, and the sexual exploitation of the women simply could not be pleasing to the God revealed in Jesus Christ and made present in power in the life of the believer through the Holy Spirit. It could not be judged a "positive good."

Complementarians are now facing exactly the same challenge. They have refused to listen to the biblical critiques of their "theology" by

1. I tell this story more fully in my *What the Bible Actually Teaches,* 180–94.
2. Knoll, *Civil War*, 2, 6, 47.
3. Knoll, *Civil War*, 54.

evangelical egalitarians for the last forty years, insisting that "what we teach is what the Bible clearly teaches," and that our headship teaching "neither supports nor fosters, but rather prevents and condemns, abuse;"[4] it is "good for women, good for children and good for families."[5] Now they are in crisis. There is an ever-growing number of first-class evangelical theologians who argue the Bible in fact makes the substantial equality of the two sexes the creation-given ideal, and the subordination of women entirely a consequence of the fall, and thus a reflection of sin.[6] And, there is ever growing hard evidence that headship teaching can encourage *some* men who go to church regularly to abuse and be violent towards their wives.[7] It is now undeniable that for large numbers of women, some married to men who identify strongly as Christians, headship teaching for them is not " benevolent," nor does it produce "holiness and happiness" in their lives.

Moore Challenges

Possibly no one has shaken complementarians in general and the Southern Baptists in particular in recent years than Beth Moore. She is possibly the best-known Southern Baptist. In 2010, *Christianity Today* called her "the most popular Bible teacher in America." She has 863 thousand Twitter followers, far in excess of any male evangelical leader.[8] As a Southern Baptist she is of course not ordained and mainly speaks to women. She has long upheld complementarian teaching. However, in the wake of the "MeToo" movement and the Paige Patterson scandal she broke ranks and wrote on May 3, 2018 an "Open Letter to My Brothers" [of complementarian conviction].[9] In this she says "she learned early to show constant pronounced deference—not just proper respect" to evangelical male leaders, and accept frequent unjustified criticism from them, and to be ignored and talked down to by these men. But in late 2016 when it emerged that key evangelical leader's views of women "smacked of misogyny, objectification and astonishing disesteem" she spoke up. She writes,

4. SBC, "On Abuse."

5. Moore, "After Patriarchy, What?," 576.

6. See Giles, *What the Bible Actually Teaches.*

7. As this book argues.

8. McAlister, "How Beth Moore is Helping Change the Face of Evangelical Leadership."

9. Moore, "Open Letter to My Brothers."

> I came face to face with one of the most demoralizing realizations of my adult life: Scripture was not the reason for this colossal disregard and disrespect of women among these many men. It was only an excuse. Sin was the reason. Ungodliness.[10]

At this point of time, she came to accept and acknowledge "that many women have experienced horrific abuses within the power structures of our [evangelical] world," and male evangelical leaders have been silent.

She then says these same evangelical leaders who have been

> quick to teach submission are often slow to point out that women were also among the followers of Christ (Luke 8), that the first recorded word out of his resurrected mouth was "woman" (John 20:15) and that same woman was the first evangelist [of the resurrection]. Many churches wholly devoted to teaching the household codes are slow to also point out the numerous women with whom the apostle Paul served and for whom he possessed obvious esteem. We are fully capable of grappling with the tension the two spectrums create and we must if we're truly devoted to the whole counsel of God's word.[11]

What is now demanded, she concludes, is a "roundtable discussion" where these issues can be faced and addressed honestly and openly.

Not unexpectedly, many read her words as a rejection and condemnation of complementarianism. Beth Allison Barr for one read it as a "recanting" of complementarianism, even though Moore does not explicitly say this. She does, however, apologize for "being part of the problem" created by complementarian teaching that demeans women, and of her "cowardly" deference to its teachers and she reminds her readers of the frequent affirmations of women and their leadership in Scripture that complementarian theologians ignore or downplay.[12]

Melani McAlister writing in the *Washington Post,* June 22, 2018, in reference to Beth Moore's letter says, "The SBC leaders are well aware that they are [now] facing a continuing crisis over how women are treated [in their churches and seminaries]. Women such as Beth Moore have started to challenge men's abuse of power."[13] She then asks, could this be the beginning of the end of the complementarian ideology? What is so

10. Moore, "Open Letter to My Brothers."

11. Moore, "Open Letter to My Brothers."

12. Barr, "Will Beth Moore Help Save Evangelicalism?"

13. McAlister, "How Beth Moore is Helping Change the Face of Evangelical Leadership."

paradoxical in this whole story is that one of the most influential leaders of the complementarian movement, Paige Patterson, who had starkly
argued for the headship of men and the submission of women for over
fifty years, was undone by women who would not be silenced. The women
he had told to "be as submissive in every way," be silent in church, and
respect the leadership of the men set over them, said to him, it's now time
for you to step down and be silent.

In 2019, just before the Dallas annual SBC meeting, Beth Moore suddenly got center stage a second time. This time it was because she tweeted
that she was planning to preach on Mother's Day. This infuriated many
Southern Baptist church leaders, who think women preaching or giving
leadership in church is sin. Her critics wrote numerous hostile responses
but large numbers of Southern Baptists supported her. In dismay Albert
Mohler, the President of the Southern Baptist Theological Seminary in
Kentucky, wrote,

> We have reached a critical moment in the Southern Baptist Con-
> vention when there are now open calls to retreat from our biblical
> convictions on complementarianism and embrace the very er-
> ror that the SBC repudiated over 30 years ago. Honestly, I never
> thought I would see this day.[14]

Sydney Anglicans

Sydney Anglicans now stand in the same existential predicament in regard to their teaching on women. They have neither been able to convince
their evangelical critics that their complementarian theology is what the
Bible teaches, nor have they been able to make any meaningful reply to
their fellow evangelicals who have rejected their interpretation of the few
verses on which they base their theology. What is more, large numbers,
if not the majority, of clergy and lay people in the diocese of Sydney are
pragmatically egalitarian. They openly admit that they have profoundly
equal marriages. The husband does not make all the important decisions,
or have "the casting vote," and the wife is not "submissive in all things."
This means there is a huge tension between what members of the diocese
are supposed to believe about the man-woman relationship and how their
marriages actually operate in most instances.

14. Mohler, "Debate Over Women's Roles."

But these are only two of the challenges facing Sydney complementarian theologians at this time. There are at least two others. In this book, I have pointed out that the best of contemporary scholarship on domestic abuse and violence makes the hierarchical ordering of the sexes the most likely predictor of this scourge. What the Sydney theologians make as the starting premise of their work on domestic abuse and violence, namely the headship of men and the submission of women, is the very thing that has to be rejected if domestic abuse and violence is to be "effectively" combatted. And then Sydney theologians are faced by the fact that Australia is a profoundly egalitarian country and women are excelling in almost every field of human endeavor. The thought that men should lead and women be submissive makes as much sense to most Australians as the claim the earth is flat. Every Australian today knows that women make excellent leaders and have exceptional gifts of communication.

This means that for Sydney Anglicans, "the woman issue" is like a wound that will not heal. It divides the church, hinders evangelism, and it never goes away. The leaders of the diocese have made their doctrine of the headship of men and the submission of women the distinctive diocesan doctrine of huge importance, arguing that it differentiates those who accept what the Bible teaches on men and women and those who do not. It is hard to see how they can come to rethink their doctrine on this matter because they have so heavily invested in it.

More than one participant in the 2018 Sydney synod debate on "the remarriage of a divorced person where the person has been abused emotionally or physically" by their husband, told me that it was obvious that the unspoken fear of the complementarian leaders of the diocese was that this motion called into question male headship and the submission of women. It did.

What is so important to note is that in the Anglican Diocese of Sydney at this time, the most outspoken supporters of complementarian teaching in the Diocese of Sydney are able women with exceptional leadership ability; women with doctorates and good theological degrees, lawyers, high school teachers, etc. They are the ones who speak publicly on this issue, put the case in print,[15] argue it online and run the "Priscilla and Aquila" conferences where the virtues of marriages where the man is the head and woman submissive and of women ministering only to women is endorsed and promulgated.[16] I have seen nothing written by

15. See Smith, *God's Good Design*; Hartley, "Evolution of the Gender Debate."
16. Priscilla and Aquila Centre.

a Sydney *male* theologian for at least twenty years, putting the comple-mentarian position. This support by able and well-qualified women of their subordinate status is hard to believe at first thought but this is the situation. What this speaks of is the power of any entrenched hierarchical ordering when it is thought that it is instituted and blessed by God him-self. In such situations (classic aristocracy, the Hindu caste system, etc.), those at the bottom of the prevailing social hierarchical ordering tend to be the most ardent supporters of the *status quo*. We see this phenomenon in the *Downton Abbey* TV series. Those "upstairs" assume their privileged position and see no need to argue for or defend it. Those "downstairs," on the other hand, vigorously argue for its maintenance and defend it. They even want to make sure the hierarchy "downstairs" among the staff is preserved. In such hierarchies, those at the top reward in various ways the defenders of their privileges who are set under them.

In the Sydney Diocese, what is most needed to bring change is for at least one of these able and strong female defenders of male headship and female submission to break ranks, like Beth Moore has in the US, and say enough is enough. Complementarian theology is neither what Scripture teaches nor something that affirms the God-given dignity and leadership of women. This will not be easy for any of these women who are now honored and praised by the diocesan leaders for upholding male leadership and female submis-sion, "as what the Bible clearly teaches." Indeed, it will be very costly for any woman now on the "inside" to do this. Like Beth Moore, she will be attacked and denigrated for her stand, and cast out of the "in group" of complementar-ians. She can only hope that the 60 percent on average of regular churchgoers who are women will in the majority support her.

For women to be set free and the abuse of women "effectively" coun-tered in the Sydney Diocese, change must come. The complementarian ideology that hierarchically orders the sexes has to be repudiated. I have done my part, and other men have tried, but I think it is now up to women to push for change by saying loudly and strongly this is *not* what the Bible clearly teaches. In creation, before the fall, God created man and woman alike in his image and likeness, and he appointed them to rule over his world standing side by side (Gen 1:27–12). The subordination of women is entirely a consequence of the fall (Gen 3:16); it is a reflection of sin. Jesus undeniably held to this pre-fall creation view of women. In his teaching and example, he said not one word on the headship of men and the submission of women and much to the contrary.[17] If we claim to be followers of Jesus we need to follow in his steps on this important matter.

P.S.

What has happened immediately prior to this book being published has underscored the importance of the topic it addresses, domestic abuse and violence. I finished writing in December 2019. While my work was being edited and set up for publishing the COVID-19 pandemic hit the world. This resulted in a second pandemic, a huge increase in the abuse of women in the home. In April 2020, the United Nations spoke of a "global upsurge" of the abuse of women and children in the over ninety countries that have instituted home lockdowns. This should not surprise us because the stressors that exacerbate abuse and violence by needy and controlling men are all present due to COVID-19; home confinement, loss of work, financial pressure, children home all day, excess drinking, etc. As a consequence, women are more at risk and there is no escape for them.

---

17. The oft-made complementarian argument that *the fact* that the twelve were all men *infers* male leadership is special pleading. Jesus's high view of women and endorsement of them in mission counters this inference (John 4:39–42; 20:18; Matt 28:10). They were also all Jews. What does this infer? The Twelve had to be men if they were to be witnesses of Jesus's ministry from the time of his baptism until his resurrection. Women in his time could not travel with him every day and sleep out under the stars with men. What is significant is that they were twelve in number signifying that Jesus was establishing the new Israel, the church. On this "inference" see Giles, *What the Bible Actually Teaches*, 87–89.

Addendum 1

Domestic Abuse: the Historical Dimension

ONE OF THE FEW benefits of age is that it gives you historical perspective. As I read everything I could on domestic abuse and violence for this book, I became aware that most of the literature was post 2000, hardly anything pre-1990, and that virtually nothing was said in this literature of what had happened in past times. In other words, it lacked an historical perspective.[1] I then recalled that for most of my active working life as a pastor/minister, beginning in 1968, I did not attend one conference or seminar on domestic abuse and violence. It was not a subject of importance to the church that demanded attention. It was no different in the wider community. Pre-1990, domestic abuse and violence got little attention in the media and there was very little in the way of legislation to protect women.

Jess Hill in her 2019, 400-page study, *See What You Made Me Do: Power, Control and Domestic Abuse,* makes the following startling comment.

> For the first time in human history we have summoned the courage to confront domestic abuse. This has been a radical shift, and in the years to come, 2014 will likely stand as the year the Western world finally started taking men's violence against women seriously.[2]

In Past Times

In past centuries, it was universally assumed that men should lead and women be submissive and obedient. Given this presupposition, it was

1. On this see Roth, "Gender, Sex and Intimate Partner Violence"; Bala, "Historical Perspective"; Hill, *See What You Made Me Do*, 2–3, 322–23; and the various sources quoted below.

2. Hill, *See What you Made Me Do*, 2.

generally accepted that a man could and should "discipline" his wife, and this could include physical punishment. Before 1850 almost every legal system in the world allowed "wife beating" as a valid exercise of a husband's authority over his wife. Before and up to the middle of the nineteenth century, wife beating in the United Kingdom was very common and only gained censure if it was exceptionally brutal and repetitive. In 1853, the first attempt at dealing with this issue was made when the all-male House of Commons passed "the Aggravated Assaults Act," seeking to stem the tide of wife beating, that one member described as "a blot upon our national character." In opposition to the Bill, Earl Granville quoted the old proverb, "A woman, a dog and a walnut tree, the more you beat them the better they be."[3] This law allowed a judge to fine a man 20 pounds, and in extreme cases jail him for six months, if convicted. Very few convictions followed and the general agreement was that little had changed. Public opinion, however, was changing, largely due to the work of "First Wave feminists" who came on the scene in the 1860s.[4] A second attempt to address wife beating in the United Kingdom was made in 1878 in "the Matrimonial Causes Act." This took jurisdiction on divorce out of the control of the church, giving it to the civil courts. The Act allowed legal separation by either a husband or a wife on grounds of adultery, cruelty, or desertion. The right to initiate divorce remained a male privilege but the court could allow a wife to separate from her husband and have custody of the children.

The story is much the same in the United States, with one notable exception. Until the middle of the nineteenth century, wife batterers were common and seldom if ever prosecuted. Judges and police struggled to know how to deter batterers whose victims were reluctant to prosecute. In 1850, Tennessee became the first state to explicitly outlaw wife beating. Other states soon followed. The one exception was the Massachusetts Bay Colony, dominated and led by English Puritans. They were ahead of everyone else. In their governing charter of 1641, "Body of Liberties of the Massachusetts Bay Colonists,"[5] it is stated that a married woman should be "free from bodilie correction by stripes by her husband."

---

3. Wojtczak, "British Women's Emancipation Since the Renaissance."

4. Giles, *What the Bible Actually Teaches*, 41.

5. "Bodies of Liberties, 1641."

More Recently

In most legal systems around the world, domestic abuse and violence only began to be seriously addressed beginning in the 1970s. In most countries before this time there was very little if any protection in law or practice for abused women. Again, feminists were to the forefront in demanding change. In the United Kingdom, three important bills marked the beginning of significant change. First, in 1978 the House of Commons passed "the Domestic Violence and Matrimonial Proceedings Act," that provided police with powers of arrest for the breach of an injunction in cases of domestic violence and allowed women to obtain the right to stay at the matrimonial home. Second, in 1978, "the Domestic Proceedings and Magistrates' Courts Act," was passed. This allowed for the giving of injunctions to prevent further violence in the home. And third, in 1977, "The Housing (Homeless Persons) Act," that aimed to help domestic violence victims with re-housing, was passed.[6] In 1971, Erin Pizzey started the first women's shelter specifically for abused women, in Chiswick, West London.

Here, I remind my readers again that the first known use of the term "domestic violence" to speak of violence in the home, was in a report to the British parliament in 1973. Before that people spoke of "wife battering."

In the US, most laws dealing with domestic abuse are state laws and as far as I can see most of these were enacted from 2000 onwards.[7] In 1994, the federal government responded to the nationwide concern about domestic and sexual violence by enacting the "Violence Against Women Act" (VAWA), designed to improve both victim services and arrest and prosecution of abusers. In 2000 and 2005 this act was revised. Another important milestone in federal legislation against domestic abuse was the 2013, "Violence Against Women Reauthorization Act." This law provided services and support for victims of domestic violence and sexual assault. The first women's shelter specifically for abused women in the United States, was established in St. Paul, Minnesota in 1972, shortly after the first domestic violence hotline was established in the same location. Soon after other shelters followed.

In Australia in 1971, "the Women's Electoral Lobby" was established to agitate for domestic abuse and rape legislation. In 1974, "Elsie," the first Australian women's shelter was established in Sydney and soon after one was

---

6. "Definitions of Domestic Violence."

7. "State and Federal Domestic Violence Laws in the United States."

begun in Melbourne. As in the United States, the Australian states and territories are primarily responsible for domestic abuse and violence legislation. Beginning in 1984, one by one, they began legislating on domestic abuse. Following the 1996 Australian Bureau of Statistics (ABS) national survey, entitled "Women's Safety Survey," which discovered very high level of abuse, John Howard, the Prime Minister, brought together the heads of all states and territories to work together on this issue. Following this meeting, the Commonwealth Government of Australia committed $50 million to test preventative measures and practices to address domestic violence.

Now to the world scene: in 1993, the United Nations published *Strategies for Confronting Domestic Violence: A Resource Manual.* This asked countries around the world to make domestic violence a criminal offence. In 1999, the United General Assembly adopted a resolution designating November 25 as the International Day for the Elimination of Violence Against Women, or White Ribbon Day. Similarly, "The Council of Europe,"[8] has undertaken a series of initiatives to promote the protection of women against violence since the 1990s. Possibly the most important has been the 2011 "Istanbul convention on preventing and combating violence against women and domestic violence." It has been signed by 44 countries.

Rape in Marriage

Nothing illustrates better how late in history social and legal change has come for abused women than the issue of "rape in marriage." For most of history, it has been believed that a wife is obligated to be sexually available to her husband, and therefore a man could not be accused of raping his wife. The view that a husband cannot be charged with the rape of his wife has long historical tradition in British common law. Sir Matthew Hale in 1736 ruled that, "The husband cannot be guilty of a rape committed by himself upon his lawful wife, for by their mutual consent and contract the wife hath given up herself in this kind unto her husband, which she cannot retract." On this view, marriage is seen as a contract for sex between spouses, no matter how a woman might feel about a particular act of intercourse. Consent was not part of the equation.

This understanding of sex in marriage only began to be seriously challenged in Western democracies in the 1960s and 70s, as second-wave

---

8. This is not to be identified with the European Union (EU). All EU countries belong to it but it has many more member countries.

feminists began making the case that women should be understood as self-determining human beings who had the right to give or not give access to their body. In Great Britain, change was initiated when a man identified only as "R" was convicted of attempting to rape his wife, but challenged the decision citing the marital rape exemption laid out by Hale. Following multiple appeals, the case eventually reached the House of Lords, which ruled against him, unanimously stating: "Nowadays it cannot seriously be maintained that by marriage a wife submits herself irrevocably to sexual intercourse in all circumstances." This led to the passing of the Sexual Offences Act of 2003 which made forced sexual intercourse within marriage a legal offence: "rape."[9]

The traditional definition of rape in the United States is forced sexual intercourse by a male with a "female *not his wife*," making it clear that a married man by definition cannot be charged with raping his wife. Pressure to rethink this issue only began to get traction in the United States in the mid-1970s. The earliest laws required that the husband and wife were not living together for marital rape charges to be brought. The case that first challenged this cohabitation clause was *Oregon v. Rideout* in 1978. Although the husband was acquitted of raping his wife, it spurred the movement towards reform. By 1993 marital rape was a crime in all 50 states.[10]

In Australia, the removal of the immunity for marital rape occurred in all states and territories, both by statute and judicial decision, between the late 1970s and early 1990s, but not without much opposition.[11]

Of all the late twentieth and early twenty-first-century marriage reforms, rape in marriage was the most divisive and opposed. It was opposed by social and religious conservatives for a number of reasons. The primary objection of evangelical religious conservatives was that it was a knife thrust at the idea of male headship and wifely submission which involved the principle that the wife should always submit to her husband's reasonable demands. Social conservatives objected because they believed that the family home, and in particular the marital bedroom, should not be controlled by the state. Other objections were the fear that it would encourage divorce, give voice to vindictive wives and it would be difficult to prove in litigation.

---

9. "Rape in Marriage."
10. "Marital Rape in the United States."
11. "Rape in Marriage: Australian Women's History Network."

The Churches

Basically, the churches have been in step with the rest of the world. Before the 1850s, church leaders tended to accept the "discipline" of wives, only speaking out against excesses and gross cruelty. In the modern period, Christians have done a little bit better—well some of them. From the 1980s, there has been a steady stream of books written by Christians addressing this problem. One early article was the 1981 essay by Susan Brooks Thistle-waite, "Battered Women and the Bible: From Subjection to Liberation."[12] In 1989, the evangelical world was rocked when James and Phyllis Alsdurf published their book, *Battered into Submission: The Tragedy of Wife Abuse in the Christian Home*. In this book, for the first time, evangelicals were confronted with the fact that Bible-believing men who went to church regularly could be, and in some cases were, abusive of and violent to their wives. Before they wrote, I do not think any evangelical had admitted that domestic abuse occurred in evangelical homes. They inspired and motivated Catherine Clark Kroeger, the founder and first president of Christians for Biblical Equality (CBE) to make further disclosures and address this scandal. She inspired and contributed to and edited a trilogy of books on domestic abuse and violence, the first appearing in 1996.[13]

One piece of good news is that the Salvation Army, long before anyone else, was active in supporting abused women. In 1883, Elizabeth Cotrill, opened her own home in East London for women in need; those escaping prostitution, homeless women, and "battered women." Later in the same year in Glasgow, the Salvation Army opened the first dedicated "Rescue Home" for women, and in London, "The Hanbury Street Refuge for Women" was opened. Also in 1883 a "Rescue Home for Women" was opened in Melbourne.[14]

At this present time, all the churches are aware of the extent of domestic abuse and violence and doing everything they can to combat it. They are seeking to inform and teach clergy and congregations on this matter, and in most cases have appointed people to lead these initiatives.

12. Thistlewaite, "Battered Women." Other early Protestant writers on the abuse of women were Nancy Nason-Clark and Marie Fortune.

13. Kroeger and Beck, *Women Abuse and the Bible*; Kroeger and Nason-Clark, *No Place for Abuse;* Nason-Clark et al., *Responding to Abuse in Christian Homes.*

14. Dr. Florey Janssen of the Heritage Centre of the Salvation Army in England and Lindsay Cox of the Australian Salvation Army supplied this information. I thank them for their help.

Action and Knowledge

For positive action to be taken to protect women, community leaders needed to be well-informed on the nature and extent of domestic abuse and violence, and this knowledge only began to become public in the post-1970 period, with the biggest advances being made after 2000. In any process of social change, knowledge and action are dynamically related and bi-directional. Thus, in tandem the law was progressively changed to protect women, and women organized shelters to protect women, as more information on domestic abuse and violence became available.[15] In the churches, this dynamic can also be seen at work. The churches have only begun to change as they have become aware of the nature and extent of domestic abuse and violence. They have not been ahead or behind any other group in society, except for feminists who have led the way, and many Christians are feminists.

And to Conclude

In this brief outline of legislative and practical measures to deal with domestic abuse and violence, I hope I have established the fact that combatting this scourge has come late in human history. What has been achieved is a result of the liberation of women—women demanding that they be respected, valued, and protected.

15. I thank Nancy Nason-Clark for this insight.

A Summary and Critical Appraisal of the Anglican Diocese of Sydney "Responding to Domestic Abuse: Policy and Good Practice" Document, Accepted and Endorsed by the 2018 Anglican Diocese of Sydney Annual Synod

THIS DOCUMENT IS A solid piece of work of 62 pages in length, compiled by twelve people, six men, six women, and chaired by Canon Sandy Grant.[1] It contains a mass of information on domestic abuse and gives clear guidelines as to how clergy should respond to this evil. It is to be highly commended for its unqualified condemnation of the abuse of women in the home or in any context and its acknowledgment that domestic abuse takes place all too often in churchgoing families, and that clergy are often offenders.

Most of what is said in the Sydney document is taken directly, often word for word, from the 2017 Church of England, "Responding Well to Domestic Abuse: Policy and Practical Guidelines," even the title except for a few minor word changes. There are, however, two very notable exceptions. First, the UK statistics on the extent of the abuse of women, which parallel closely what I consider to be the accurate Australian statistics,[2] are replaced by another set of statistics that do not refer specifically to domestic abuse and suggest that a significant percentage of women are guilty of domestic abuse, and second, the egalitarian reading of Scripture given in the English document is replaced by a complementarian reading of Scripture.[3]

---

1. Kara Hartley kindly sent me electronically a copy of this document, but it is available on the internet. See Anglican Diocese of Sydney, "Responding."

2. Church of England, "Responding Well," 27. On my discussion and conclusions on Australian statistics, see chapter 1 of this book.

3. Church of England, "Responding Well," 43–44.

Because the Sydney document is so heavily dependent on its English counterpart, much of it is uncontroversial and good sound common sense. There is, however, much in the Sydney document that needs to be critically evaluated and contested. Here we note it was an "in house" project. All the members of the task force were appointed by the leaders of the Diocese of Sydney, and the chair Canon Sandy Grant and the deputy chair, Kara Hartley, are "card-carrying" convinced complementarians. They determined what went in the document. Most members of the working party did not identify themselves as complementarians, and at least two saw themselves as "evangelical egalitarians." What is more, there were members of the task force with considerable experience in responding to victims of abuse, and well-informed on the scholarly work on domestic abuse. However, all of them were constrained by the motion of synod, setting up the task force. It required the committee to address domestic abuse on the basis of an unquestioned commitment to "a complementarian framework" of male headship and female submission.[4]

I sent this addendum in draft to three members of the task force for critical evaluation. Each one asked for a few factual matters to be corrected, which I did. One of them made the point very strongly that this document represents a huge step forward for Sydney Anglicans. For the first time it has been publicly acknowledged that abuse and violence in church homes is far too common and clergy have been offenders. And as a result, clear guidelines are given in this document, ratified by synod, as to how clergy are to respond to reports of abuse and how offending clergy are to be disciplined and their wives supported. This respondent to my work said,

> I joined this task force because I wanted to see the issue of domestic abuse and violence in Sydney Diocese addressed and dealt with. I wanted to get a policy on abuse instituted in the diocese that would help our churches respond in a more informed way. For me, the issue was not theology, but how to get something concrete done that would guide us to better recognise and support victims of domestic abuse and to hold perpetrators of that abuse accountable.

I fully concede the point. Nothing in what follows should be taken to minimize the huge importance of what this task force has achieved. It represents an epochal change in the Sydney Diocese. The Diocese has now conceded

---

4. "Sydney Synod Responds to Domestic Abuse."

that domestic abuse and violence in the homes of Sydney churchgoers and clergy is far too common; it is sinful, and it must be countered rigorously.

Now the Document

Archbishop Glenn Davies in his foreword says,

> God's word condemns unloving behavior, and especially the misuse of power to control or exploit others. Abuse in all its forms is explicitly forbidden, as it is contrary to the nature of God and the love that he demands of us all. Yet sadly, not all husbands love their wives as Christ loved the Church, nor do all wives love their husbands as they should.
>
> The effects of sin are ever present, and can cause great havoc to otherwise healthy relationships. For these reasons, we are concerned for those relationships where domestic abuse is present. We wish to address this issue honestly and transparently; we also wish to extend our care and compassion to those who suffer domestic abuse.
>
> This is a sensitive area for us to explore, but it must be explored and exposed, so that we might live as children of light, seeking to honor Christ as Lord and Savior in every community, especially the family.

Then follow the aims of this study.

> This document sets out the Domestic Abuse Policy and Good Practice Guidelines of the Anglican Diocese of Sydney, as evidence and expression of the Church's commitment to address and *respond effectively* to domestic abuse both within its own community and in the wider society. (Italics added)

In this introductory section, the authors say they prefer the term, "domestic abuse," because domestic abuse concerns far more than physical violence. I agree entirely.

In sections 1.1 to 1.8 this document acknowledges that domestic abuse can take place in churchgoing families and clergy can be perpetrators. And, it gives guidelines as to how the church and clergy in particular should respond to women who have experienced domestic abuse.

In section 1.9, titled "Thinking Theologically," we are given "10 statements on domestic abuse." These include an affirmation of the equal dignity and worth of men and women and of the God-ordained nature of marriage.

Separation from an abusive husband is allowed, but divorce on this basis is not endorsed. Sections 1.10 and 1.11 give helpful advice on how to respond to accusations of domestic abuse. Section 1.12 gives a "flowchart" on the progressive steps to be taken when an accusation of domestic abuse is made and section 1.13 gives the telephone numbers in Sydney that may be needed.

Section 2 is titled, "Addressing domestic abuse: good practice guidelines." It begins with this definition of domestic abuse.

> Domestic abuse is defined as abusive or intimidating behavior inflicted by an adult against a current or former spouse or partner. It includes, but is not limited to, emotional, verbal, social, economic, psychological, spiritual, physical and sexual abuse. Such behavior often seeks to control, humiliate, dominate or instill fear in the victim.

Following next, helpful advice is given on how to respond to cases of abuse, much of it repeating what has been said in section 1. Pastors, ordained or lay, are to listen, accept what is said, inform the police, make sure children are safe if they are involved, check that the woman has a refuge, and keep a record of what was said and what was done. Sections 2.12 and 13 deal specifically with the response needed when a clergyman is accused of domestic abuse.

Section 3 is titled "Appendices." I list the topics discussed.

1. An expansive description of Domestic Abuse

2. The Duluth 'Power and Control' Wheel

3. Domestic Abuse Facts

    i. Who experiences domestic abuse?

    ii. Domestic Abuse Statistics for Australia

    iii. Challenging misconceptions about domestic abuse

    iv. Recognizing domestic abuse in adult victims

    v. Recognizing domestic abuse in children

    vi. Who are the perpetrators of domestic abuse?

    vii. Recognizing perpetrators of domestic abuse

    viii. Particular Types of Domestic abuse

4. Legal Framework

5. Domestic Abuse: Policy Guidance from *Faithfulness in Service*

6. Suggested Parish Policy on Domestic Abuse

7. Draft Safety and Exit plan

8. Marriage Preparation: Recommended good practice

9. Synod Resolutions related to Domestic Abuse

10. Timeline of Public Statements by Diocesan Leadership addressing Domestic Abuse

11. "A Letter Made Me Think"

12. "Walking Through It: A Family Violence Survivor's Reflection"

13. Doctrine Commission on Divorce and Remarriage

14. Doctrine Commission on The Use and Misuse of Scripture with Regard to Domestic Abuse.

Most of the material in this section invites no comment. Some of it is factual information and some good pastoral advice. At this point I will only question the section on statistics.

Before I do this, I note that the statistics are introduced by this comment,

> Statistics do not tell the whole story, as they do not identify patterns of control and abuse in relationships. They do not capture level of fear, or the severity of injury or impact, for the victim."[5]

This is a very helpful comment but I must add that differing statistics on any given matter tell differing stories.

On page 27 of the Sydney document we are told that,

- 1 in 6 women (17 percent) and 1 in 16 men (6 percent) had experienced threatened or actual physical or sexual violence by a partner they had lived with.

- 23 percent of women and 16 percent of men have experienced emotional abuse by a partner since the age of 15.

- Most (69 percent) of domestic assault victims are women, but almost one-third involved a male victim.

The statistics in the Church of England, "Responding Well" document are,

---

5. Anglican Diocese of Sydney, "Responding," 27.

> Two women are killed every week in England and Wales by current or former partners (Office of National Statistics, 2015)—1 woman killed every 3 days. · 1 in 4 women in England and Wales will experience domestic violence in their lifetimes and 8% will suffer domestic violence in any given year (Crime Survey of England and Wales, 2013/14).[6]

We first immediately notice that the number of women killed each week is missing from the Sydney statistics. In Australia, with a much smaller population, one woman a week is killed by her intimate partner.[7] Next, we note the English figures say 1 in 4 women will experience domestic violence in their lifetime. The Sydney document says, "1 in 6 women (17%) and 1 in 16 men (6%)." Finally, we note the Sydney document next gives two sets of figures, reflecting the last words of the quote just given, suggesting that men are just a bit worse when it comes to domestic abuse and violence than women. Nothing like this is found in the Church of England report.

The Sydney statistics come from the 2016 Australian Bureau of Statistics (ABS), "personal safety review." They are statistics on "partner violence," not "domestic abuse." Later this ABS document gives the figure for "partner emotional abuse" as 1 in 4 women. This is the widely endorsed figure for *domestic abuse* in the Western world, the figure given in the English report, and the figure I endorse in chapter 1.[8] The next two sets of statistics given by the ABS and quoted in the Sydney document are equally confusing and

---

6. Church of England, "Responding Well," 27.

7. Kara Hartley, in responding to my work, pointed out that the number of women killed is given on the next page of the Sydney document, but this long section is so convoluted in wording you would never conclude that one woman a week is killed by her partner. I read this section several times and found it opaque.

8. I give again my sources for this conclusion from chapter 1. For my statistics on the world scene, I followed Heise and Kotsadam, "Cross-National and Multilevel Correlatives of Partner Violence." On the US, I consulted "Violence Against Women in the United States," and, "Domestic Violence Statistics." For Australia, my sources were Hill, *See What You Made Me Do;* "Change the Story"; and the Australian Institute of Health and Welfare, "Family, Domestic and Sexual Violence in Australia." Hill, *See What You Made Me Do,* 4n**, contests rightly the "one in six" figure quoted in some publications. *Our Watch* is an Australian group that has been established to drive nationwide change in behaviors and power imbalances that lead to violence against women and their children. They give the following figures: 1 in 3 Australian women have experienced physical violence since the age of 15; 1 in 4 Australian women have experienced physical or sexual violence by an intimate partner, and 1 in 5 Australian women have experienced sexual violence ("Change the Story"). The Australian Institute of Health and Welfare report also gives the figure, 1 in 4 women have experienced abuse from an intimate partner.

unhelpful. Men and women verbally abuse each other in close numbers and men and women can hit and hurt each other but this is not, I say yet again, "domestic abuse." This is what is often called "situational violence."

In discussing *domestic abuse*, it must be perfectly clear that we are focusing on a carefully defined phenomenon, rightly defined in this document on p. 14.

> Domestic abuse is defined as abusive or intimidating behavior inflicted by an adult against a current or former spouse or partner. It includes, but is not limited to, emotional, verbal, social, economic, psychological, spiritual, physical and sexual abuse. Such behavior often seeks to control, humiliate, dominate or instill fear in the victim.

Such behavior is *almost* exclusively gender specific. Women as a general rule cannot intimidate or instill fear in a man. Women as a general rule do not exercise financial control and so it is women who are economically disempowered and disadvantaged when they leave. Men seldom if ever flee the home with their children in fear of their life and women do not inflict sexual violence on men. True, women sometimes kill their intimate partner but almost always as a result of years of violence that has been soul destroying.

When it comes to periodic or occasional acts of abuse or violence, "situational violence," in couple relationships, the statistics for men and women do come close together. Women are almost as likely to speak abusively and even hit their husband in anger as a man. But this is *not* domestic abuse, as the definition just given makes clear.

But it is not only that the Sydney statistics supposedly on *domestic abuse* are unhelpful to say the least, it is clear they are given to suggest that perpetrators of domestic abuse can *often* be women. This suggestion appears elsewhere in this document. Twice we are told that, "Sometimes both spouses can be simultaneously perpetrators and victims of abuse, although neither is the pattern of abuse nor the impact generally symmetrical" (3 and 27). I have seen no similar claim in any of the scientific literature. Indeed, such claims are strongly rejected as untrue by most experts on domestic abuse. This kind of claim comes directly from literature put out by members of the so-called "men's movement."[9] It said to deny that domestic abuse is almost invariably gender specific; essentially male. A similar yet

---

9. See publications by the Australian group "One in Three" for such statements. In reply, see "Domestic Violence in Australia," Australia's National Research Organization for Women's Safety (ANROW).

more balanced relativizing statement is found on page 27, "Most domestic abuse is perpetrated by men against women, but the perpetrator of domestic abuse can be of either sex, and the victim can be of either sex." In the several places where clergy abuse is mentioned, not once is gender mentioned, yet in the Sydney Diocese only men can be in charge of a parish. All the examples of abuse by clergy within the diocese have involved male clergy abusing their wives. This fact is neatly sidestepped.

What Is Exceptional in this Document and Most Problematic

One thing categorically sets this response to domestic abuse apart from all the other reports, studies, and books I read on this issue. In this study alone the premise is that men should lead and women be "submissive." Despite the fact that "Research has consistently found that men who hold traditional, hierarchical views about gender roles and relationships are more likely to perpetuate violence against women,"[10] the Sydney document endorses the hierarchical ordering of the sexes, never questioning it!

Twenty-three times this document speaks of "the headship" of men and of "the submission of women," and twenty-five times it says that the Bible teaches that a wife is to "submit" to her husband. There is no ambiguity in these statements although what is being said is obfuscated by the fact that twenty-two times the document speaks of the "equality" of men and women, and once of their "profound equality." These are empty and self-serving affirmations of "equality." This document is predicated on a "complementarian framework" in which women because they are women and for no other reason are set under men—they are to be submissive and submit. They are not equals in any substantive sense. Mark Thompson, without recognizing it, allows that his assertion of the "equality" of the sexes is vacuous when he says men and women have an "asymmetrical relation as equals."[11] The word "asymmetrical" means similar but not the same! These affirmations of "equality" of course refer only to spiritual equality, or equality of worth in God's eyes; they have no practical content in everyday life. In any substantive sense, men and women are not equal; men because they are men are to lead; women because they are women are to be "submissive." This repeated affirmation of male-female "equality" quite frankly is disingenuous. Men and women are "equal" but men are more equal! I ask the authors of *The*

10. "Change the Story," 25.
11. "Sydney Synod Responds to Domestic Abuse," 51.

Sydney Anglican Policy on Responding to Domestic Abuse, "If women are equal before God, why are they not equal before men?"

It is worth noting at this point that the Sydney document speaks consistently of the "submission" of women. This word is their rendering into English of the Greek verb, *hypotassō,* which Peter O'Brien says is "a strong word" that should be rendered "be subordinate." It implies one party "has authority over another."[12] In Eph 5:21 we have the present middle/passive participle form of the verb, *hypotassomenai,* but O'Brien argues that when it is carried over to verse 22 it should be read as an imperative, *be subordinate.*[13] In many English versions of Eph 5:22 the verb is translated, "Wives be subject to your husbands" (RSV, NRSV, NAB), or "wives submit to your husbands" (NKJ, NIV, Good News). It seems the working party on abuse wanted to soften the force of the verb, possibly to make their teaching more palatable to the modern ear.

The hierarchical ordering of the sexes, this document claims, is what the Bible clearly teaches and therefore it must be obeyed; it must be good for men and women and it cannot in any way encourage or legitimate the abuse of women. I now give examples of this reasoning in the document, some attributed to specific people, without comment. I think they speak for themselves. In most of these quotes, in direct contradiction to the prevailing scholarly opinion, the claim is made that teaching the headship of men and the "submission" of women, the hierarchical ordering of the sexes, in no way encourages or legitimates domestic abuse and violence. Those quoted seem to think that by boldly and forcefully denying this connection all research to the contrary is negated!

> Any attempt to justify abusive behavior by the use of passages in the Bible which speak of headship and submission is intolerable. (p. 6)
>
> Synod affirms that the relationship of loving, sacrificial leadership of a husband and the intelligent, voluntary submission of a wife is the Biblical pattern of marriage, and totally rejects the use of this Biblical to justify any form of domestic abuse. (p. 47)
>
> Synod requests Moore College and Ministry Training and Development, . . . to develop an effective approach to educating ordinands and clergy in regards to domestic violence and how to respond when it comes up as an issue in marriage (and other relationships). In such training, consideration ought to be given

12. O'Brien, *Ephesians,* 411.

13. O'Brien, *Ephesians,* 411.

to ensuring that upholding *the Bible's good teaching on submission* and sacrificial love—both in preaching and teaching, and in marriage education and counselling. (p. 48)

Of course, domestic abuse can occur whether the theory you espouse is 'traditional', 'egalitarian' or 'feminist'. But whatever you understand when the Bible talks of 'submission' or being the 'head in a marriage', it's crystal clear that husbands are never told to make their wives submit. (p. 51.)

We began . . . by recognizing that in recent days attempts have been made to draw a causal connection between the biblical teaching about a wife's submission to her husband and the scourge of domestic violence. The charge has been made that this doctrine encourages the subjugation of women and allows a justification for abuse in all its forms. . . . there is nothing in Scripture which justifies the use of violence towards women or the abuse of women in any way whatsoever, and whenever an appeal is made to Scripture in attempt to justify such behavior it is not only a perversion of Scripture, but a dishonoring of the God whose word it is.

Far from being an embarrassment to Christian men and women at the beginning of the twenty-first century, this biblical teaching is something we should rejoice in, because it is God's word to us and God is good and always provides for the welfare of his people. We need to speak out in the loudest possible voices against domestic violence and do all in our power to protect those who have been subjected to it — women and men — I hope we will all do that and continue to do that. *But biblical headship and submission is not the cause, in fact quite the opposite.* (p. 51, quoting Mark Thompson, Principal of Moore Theological College. Italics in the last line are added. He was not on the committee. His words are simply quoted with approval.)

Passages like Ephesians 5 encourage women to submit to their husbands; is there a risk these passages can be used to excuse domestic violence? Yes, they may be used to justify sinful behavior like domestic violence. Yet we must be clear, the instruction for women to submit to their husbands does not give license to men to exploit or abuse their wives. In fact, the wife's submission is voluntary. The truth is that as women are called to submit in Ephesians 5, husbands are instructed to love their wives as they love their own bodies.

There is a lot of discussion at the moment suggesting there is a link between biblical teaching on submission and headship with the prevalence of DV in church. Some argue the existence of this teaching leads to domestic violence. I believe this is mistaken for two reasons. Firstly, to create cause and effect at this point suggests that God's good word to us is wrong or mistaken. Also, taken to its logical conclusion, it would assume that churches that deny this teaching are free from DV which we know is untrue. Secondly, by making this the reason for DV means we fail to fully explore and understand the issue and that, I think, is an injustice to those involved.

Church leaders have a responsibility to teach this doctrine correctly, call out inappropriate and sinful misapplications, and care for those who have suffered at the hands of those who have (wickedly) twisted God's word to satisfy their own sinful behavior. (p. 52–53, quoting, the deputy chair of the document, Kara Hartley.)

For me, these assertions that the Bible clearly teaches that God has given men "headship" and women are to be "submissive," and the bland denials that the hierarchical ordering of the sexes is the root cause of domestic abuse and violence are deeply troubling. I see them as *spiritual abuse*—the use of the Bible to maintain male privilege and deny empirical research. Every one of these authors of this document knows that most of the church, including very large numbers of evangelical biblical scholars, are of another opinion on what the Bible teaches on the man-woman relationship. These scholars argue that the "complementarian position," endorsed by this document, is *not* what the Bible clearly teaches. The Bible in fact clearly teaches the unqualified equality of the two bodily differentiated sexes as the creation ideal and as a faithful reflection of the teaching and example of Jesus Christ. For substantiation of this assertion, I say again, you may like to read my book, *What the Bible Actually Teaches On Women* (Cascade, 2018). The argument that the Bible in fact makes the essential equality of the sexes the creation ideal, the subordination of women being entirely a consequence of the fall, is so compelling that I am not expecting any answer.

The Ordination Issue

Nothing is said in this document on the fact that in the Diocese of Sydney, women cannot be ordained as an Anglican priest and thus they cannot be pastors of churches. In Sydney, all the bishops (one archbishop and six assistant bishops), all the theological lecturers at Moore Theological College, and all those in charge of a church/parish are men. Women are restricted to working with women and children and to pastoral care. This prohibition on women in church leadership is based on the dogmatic principle that God has appointed men to lead and women to be submissive. For a woman to be in charge of a church and preach/teach would abrogate this principle. At first thought this would seem inconsequential for any discussion on the abuse of women, but this is not the case. Excluding women from leadership in the church today when, in every other sphere of modern life, they are in leadership positions and excelling is a huge problem. It says loud and clear that women are second-class church members. Men are born to be leaders; women are not. Such thinking is fertile soil for the abuse of women to occur.

To adequately and effectively counter this implied low view of women, women need to be accepted for ordination and this can be done by a vote of the Sydney Synod. Lowik and Taylor say,

> The culture of male privilege in evangelical Christian communities can be changed with more women positioned as senior ministers. This move can disrupt notions that men have authority over women, and mean problems that affect women might no longer be overlooked.[14]

It is almost universally agreed today that political parties, businesses, the professions, the police force—need I go on?—are all more productive and healthier when the leadership abilities of women are recognized and affirmed, and all positions of authority are open to them. We also know that where women are excluded from leadership, organizations do not perform at their optimum and dysfunctional behavior occurs. Why should it be different in the church?

Women in church leadership is not an evil. From their inception in 1865, the Salvation Army has enshrined in its constitution gender equality. Men and women in partnership lead churches. The Salvation Army is the most respected church in the modern world because it puts into practice what it teaches. The Pentecostals are the most vibrant and fastest growing churches and they make spiritual gifting not gender the prerequisite to lead a church and preach. And today, most Anglican dioceses accept women for ordination and are glad they do so.

The Diocese of Sydney cannot adequately or effectively deal with domestic abuse in its ranks until it deals with the issue of the principled exclusion of women from church leadership. This implies a devaluation of

---

14. Lowik and Taylor, "Evangelical Churches Believe Men Should Control Women."

women; that Sydney Diocese has a low view of women. I say again, such a context is fertile soil for the abuse of women to occur.

What is so important to recognize is that men exclude women from ordination to preserve their own power and control of the church, and a theology to validate this conclusion is then developed. For evangelicals, this theology is predicated on the idea that in creation before the fall God set the man over the woman; for Roman Catholics this theology is predicated on the idea that the twelve apostles were the first priests and the twelve apostles were men. The Roman Catholic Church rejects the idea that in creation before the fall God set the man over the woman. With egalitarian evangelicals, they hold that the subordination of women is entirely a consequence of the fall, and should be opposed by Christians.[15]

Now the worrying parallel: men exclude women from ordination, using different arguments to preserve their own power; men abuse women because they believe they should have power over them. They should be in control and make all the important decisions.

The Problem

I am sure at this point we all see the problem. The Anglican Diocese of Sydney's belief that men because they are men, and for no other reason, are to lead in the home and the church, and women because they are women, and for no other reason, are to be "submissive," or, "submit to their husband," would seem to approve and legitimate what virtually all social scientists hold is the root cause of domestic abuse; the belief that men should rule over women; the denial of her essential equality.

Reiterating what I say in the body of my book I quote five examples of the prevailing scholarly opinion:

> Jess Hill: "It is indisputable that traditional notions of masculinity—particularly male entitlement—are at the core of men's violence against women."[16]

> Liz Wall: [In domestic abuse and violence] "the vital element to consider is the gender norms and beliefs surrounding male

---

15. John-Paul II, *Mulierus Dignitatem*, 88.
16. See Hill, *See What You Made Me Do*, 109.

dominance and male superiority, created by power hierarchies that accord men greater status."[17]

Our Watch: "Research has consistently found that men who hold traditional, hierarchical views about gender roles and relationships are more likely to perpetuate violence against women."[18]

The Lancet: "The main drivers of partner violence are gender related norms and hierarchies that shape relationships between men and women."[19]

Steven Tracy: (An evangelical theologian who says he is a "soft complementarian.") "Models of patriarchy which give husbands the greatest levels of power and authority are most likely to stimulate domestic violence."[20] And, "there is abundant data showing that conceptions of gender in which males are viewed as superior to females and in which males are attributed greater power to control females are predictors of increased levels of domestic violence.[21]

Missing from this Diocese of Sydney document, "Responding to Domestic Abuse," is an *extended* discussion on what causes *some men* to abuse their wives. However, throughout the document, almost as if the authors do not realize what they are saying, the scholarly opinion, just given, is endorsed. Archbishop Davies, on p. 1 says, "God's word condemns unloving behavior, and especially the misuse of power to control or exploit others." On page 3 we are told, the abuser "seeks to control, humiliate, dominate or instill fear in the victim." On p. 4, "Abuse of power is at the heart of many relationship problems in the Church and in the community. In essence, abuse is one person's misuse of power over another." On p. 28, domestic "abuse happens because an abusive person chooses to behave in a way that enables them to assert power and control over another person—excuses and reasons are given to justify abusive behavior." On p. 31, "Whatever the contributors in any given case, domestic abuse *always* involves a misuse of power by one person over another. Individuals who perpetrate domestic abuse generally do so to get what they want and to

---

17. Wall, "Gender Equality and Violence Against Women," 2.

18. "Change the Story," 25.

19. Heise and Kotsadam, "Cross-National and Multilevel Correlates of Partner Violence," 336. This is put as a thesis to be tested. It is found correct by the research.

20. Tracy, "Patriarchy and Domestic Abuse," 42.

21. Tracy, "Asking Christians to Do Better."

gain control." On p. 37, "the *misuse of power* is at the heart of abuse. This includes domestic abuse."

At this point we should all hear the bells ringing. The Diocese of Sydney's document, "Responding to Domestic Abuse," unambiguously teaches that men are head-over women and women are to be submissive and yet it acknowledges in passing that domestic abuse "*always* involves a misuse of power by one person over another." Headship teaching of course does not make all men abusive; most men are not abusive and virtually by definition a "happy" marriage today is a profoundly equal relationship, even for those who call themselves "complementarians." However, when headship teaching is heard by needy and controlling men, of which there are many in our churches, and among the clergy, they think that they should be in control; they should be obeyed. They assert their power over their wife at great cost to her, believing this is what the Bible wants them to do. Headship teaching in their ears encourages them to be abusive to get their own way, and it legitimates their behavior.

When the Diocese of Sydney began discussing the setting up of a task force on domestic abuse, following the press articles by Julia Baird and Hayley Mills, exposing the extent of abuse in the church, some of it by clergy, the Executive Officer of Rape and Domestic Violence Services in Australia, Karen Willis, said in response,

> Gender inequity leads to a culture where people feel a sense of entitlement and the right to tell another individual what to do. It also results in a culture of strict gender roles and sexual stereotyping. These are some of the issues which underpin sexual assault and domestic violence. My feeling is that the [Anglican] Church [in Sydney] may want to look closely at its own structure and teachings in this regard as a starting point if it is serious about addressing domestic violence in the community.[22]

As we have just seen, this is the very thing the task force refused to do.

And the Dire Consequences

The Sydney diocesan task force on domestic abuse and violence, we are told in the document, had as its aim, "to address and *respond effectively* to domestic abuse both within its own community [the Anglican Church in

---

22. Brown, "Sydney Anglican Church Addresses Domestic Abuse."

Sydney] and in the wider society." It certainly laid down some good practical guidelines on how abuse in churchgoing families and clergy families should be addressed but in the end it did not "*respond effectively* to domestic abuse . . . within its own community" because it endorsed the hierarchical ordering of the sexes, the root cause of domestic abuse and violence. Let me quote Liz Wall and Carrie Yodanis again. First, Liz Wall:

> A lack of gender equality is consistently cited as an underlying determinant of violence against women. The United Nations General Assembly, in its 1993 Declaration on the Elimination of Violence Against Women, noted that this violence is a manifestation of historically unequal power relations between men and women. Gender inequality as a cause of violence against women also underpins approaches to prevention by organizations such as the World Health Organization and, in Australia, VicHealth, as well as much of the research on the topic. *Achieving gender equality is the key goal in the prevention of violence against women by those aiming to reduce gender violence.*[23]

And now Carrie Yodanis, who says for more than thirty years scholars have agreed:

> In order to stop men's use and women's experience of violence on the personal level, structures of gender inequality at the societal level must change. . . . Gender inequality, or patriarchy, is both ideological (the beliefs, norms, and values about the status and roles of women in society) and structural (women's access to positions of leadership within social institutions).[24]

Conclusion

This Sydney document addressing domestic abuse and violence in my mind is like a document prepared to address climate change. Everything needing to be known about weather patterns, rising land and sea temperatures, and the consequences of these changes are given in great detail. It is emphatically stated that the continual rise in temperatures is catastrophic. It has to be stopped. However, the one thing that almost all the experts agree on is that the primary cause, the burning of fossil fuels by human beings, is openly endorsed and commended.

23. Wall, "Gender Equality and Violence Against Women," 2. Italics added.
24. Yodanis, "Gender Inequality," 655–56.

Addendum 3

"Headship teaching does not encourage or legitimate domestic abuse and violence."

WHEN I HAD FINISHED this book in first draft, I sent an electronic copy to ten people, asking them to critically read my manuscript or parts of it where I had quoted them. My complementarian respondents all sought to refute or play down the charge that complementarian headship teaching can lead to abuse in churchgoing evangelical families and in the mind of the abuser legitimate their behavior. They offered five alternative answers, sometimes mentioning just one, more often several. In most cases they told me confidently that headship teaching in fact countered abuse. I have touched on all these replies at some point earlier in this book, but I give my answers yet one more time.

1. *Domestic abuse and violence is just as common in churches with an egalitarian pastor as ones with a complementarian pastor.* In my correspondence with complementarian leaders in the Diocese of Sydney I was told this almost in every email and conversation. It is certainly true that domestic abuse and violence can be found in non-Christian and Christian homes, and in churches with a complementarian pastor and in ones with an evangelical egalitarian pastor. I led five churches in my 50 years of ministry and in every one I had couples where this was an issue. In every case, I discovered the man had very different ideas about marriage than I did. Most of them had imbibed strong headship teaching as young men in other churches or in their university evangelical student group.

The premise behind this argument is that what the pastor teaches and what the people in the church think and do correspond. This is of course not true. People in the pew have minds of their own and on numerous things they may well differ from their pastor. This "slippage" between what is taught by the minister/pastor and what the people in the pew believe and do must be allowed to be the case also in churches where there is an evangelical egalitarian pastor. What is more, I agree with complementarians that in most cases the headship teaching of pastors does not lead to most men being abusive and controlling. They hear this teaching frequently yet they have profoundly equal marriages. The man does not make all the important decisions or have the "casting vote."

The argument that there is a significance difference in the incidence of domestic abuse and violence between churches where complementarian teaching is well-entrenched and churches where egalitarian teaching is well-entrenched is strong and cannot be summarily dismissed. No research of any substance has been done on this question because evangelical churches have not wanted it and have not supported it. Nevertheless, there is evidence for this thesis. The incidence of domestic abuse and violence in the SBC and among Sydney Anglicans, where complementarian teaching is the prevailing dogma, is exceptionally high.

Then we have the fact that the scholarly consensus today is that the drivers that lead men to abuse their wives are the same for all men. Most importantly is a belief in male privilege; the belief that men are to lead, women are to be submissive. This being the case, surely we can safely infer that telling families week after week "the Bible clearly teaches that the man should lead and the woman be submissive, and the man should make all the important decisions" is *heady* stuff that can lead *some* men inclined to be controlling and abusive to seek to put this teaching into practice. And conversely, surely telling husbands and wives week after week that they should treat each other as substantial equals, love each other like Christ loved the church, they have both been given the Holy Spirit in like measure, and therefore alike have ministries in the church, and that mutual subordination is distinctive in the Christian understanding of marriage, powerfully discourage abuse and violence in the home.

2. *It's not biblical headship teaching that encourages and legitimates domestic abuse and violence but distorted or misunderstood headship teaching that has this outcome.* Next in frequency, I was told by complementarians that it is not what we teach that causes *some* men in our churches to be abusive and violent, it is a distortion of what we teach that is the

problem. What is more I was told repeatedly that headship teaching has the opposite effect, it counters domestic abuse and violence.[1]

In reply to this defense I ask, do not you complementarians explicitly, openly, and consistently teach that the husband should be in charge and wives should be submissive, as Paul says, "in all things" (Eph 5:24), and the man should make all the major decisions? And do you not teach explicitly, openly, and consistently that men and women have been given "different roles" in creation that can never change; men have the leading "role," women the submissive "role"? If no denial can be made, and in all honesty, what has just been said cannot be denied, then headship teaching *as it is given* is a huge problem. It can be toxic for many marriages. Another problem for this answer is that in the Diocese of Sydney and in the Southern Baptist Convention, a disproportionate number of abusers have been trained theologians with a comprehensive understanding of Scripture. In the SBC, 380 clergy were found to be abusers! Most of these offenders in Australia and America would hold a master's degree in theology. Apparently, they all thought Scripture authorized their behavior and legitimated it.

3. *Teaching that husbands should lead and make all the important decisions and that wives are to be submissive cannot be the cause of domestic abuse and violence because just as many women, or almost as many women, abuse their husbands.* This is another very common answer I heard. It is simply not true. A clear and sharp distinction has to be made between "situational abuse and violence" that is occasional and non-gender specific, and domestic abuse which is ongoing and almost entirely a male sin. Yes, on occasions of stress and frustration women can lose their temper and speak abusively to their husbands, hit them in anger or throw something at them. This is "situational abuse." It is is not domestic abuse or domestic violence as defined by virtually every expert in this field, including the authors of the Sydney Diocesan Response to Domestic Abuse. Domestic abuse and violence by definition always involves two things: one party seeks to exercise power and control over the other party, systematically and comprehensively, and one party lives in fear. Lundy Bancroft says "I reserve

---

1. So Mark Thompson, the Principal of Moore Theological College, Sydney. He says, "Biblical headship and submission is not the cause [of domestic abuse], *in fact quite the opposite.*" Anglican Diocese of Sydney, "Responding," 51. Italics added. In the body of this book I give several other quotes by complementarians saying the same thing.

the word [domestic] *abuse* for situations of control and intimidation."[2] White Ribbon, Australia defines it this way. "Domestic violence refers to violence, abuse and intimidation between people who are currently or have previously been in an intimate relationship. The perpetrator uses violence to control and dominate the other person. This causes fear, physical harm and/or psychological harm."[3] Jess Hill gives a more descriptive definition, "Domestic abuse is not just violence. It's worse. It is a unique phenomenon, in which the perpetrator takes advantage of their partner's love and trust and uses that persons most intimate details—their deepest desires, shames and secrets—as a blueprint for their abuse."[4] Lastly, I give the definition in the Sydney Diocesan response to domestic abuse. "Domestic abuse includes but is not limited to emotional, verbal, social, economic, psychological, spiritual, physical and sexual abuse. Such behavior often seeks to control, humiliate, dominate or instill fear in the victim."[5] Women as a general rule cannot and do not exercise coercive power and control over men, and men as a general rule do not live in constant fear of their partner/wife, and they do not flee the home with their children in trepidation. To my knowledge there are no men's shelters, established to protect men fleeing from a violent wives. In almost every case where a woman kills her partner, she does so in response to awful violence against her.

4. *The biblical idea that men should be in charge, the patriarchal principle, cannot be the problem because in the Nordic countries, where the equality of the sexes has huge support, domestic abuse and violence remain at very high levels, the highest levels in the Western democracies.* In answer, I say, this is exactly what we should expect. The emancipation and empowerment of women makes needy and controlling men very angry as they see their power being undermined in their own home. They become more determined to hold onto the power they have. It creates a backlash. In many immigrant families we see this also. Domestic abuse and violence increases when they come to their new home in the West. Wives find freedoms and power they had never imagined in their homeland, and their husbands feel they are losing power and become abusive.

2. Bancroft, *Why Does He Do That?*, 129.
3. "Domestic Violence Definition."
4. Hill, *See What You Made Me Do*, 6.
5. Anglican Diocese of Sydney, "Responding," 3.

5. *Abuse and violence is only a problem in homes where the man is an irregular churchgoer.*[6] This explanation is no longer plausible. In recent times, in the Southern Baptist Convention and in the Anglican Diocese of Sydney, both dogmatically complementarian churches, it has been discovered that the worst abusers attend church regularly and are often clergy. Pastors go to church every week! In Australia this answer does not work because by and large we have very few, if any, male irregular churchgoers, and even less that quote the Bible to justify their behavior. In contemporary Aussie culture, if you are not a committed Christian you don't go to church as a general rule.

6. This argument was put first 12 years ago by the American theologian, Steven Tracy, in "Patriarchy and Domestic Abuse," and taken up later by Wilcox, "Evangelicals and Domestic Abuse." Complementarians repeat this argument incessantly. It has no validity whatsoever. Regular churchgoing men are in fact serious offenders. Most telling is that two social scientists, Naomi Priest and Nicolas Biddle, evaluated the claims made by Tracy and Wilcox and found them unsubstantiated. See Priest and Biddle, "The Verdict on Domestic Violence Data and the Church."

Bibliography

"100 Verses on Domestic Abuse and Violence." *OpenBible Info*. https://www.openbible. info/topics/domestic_violence_and_abuse.

"Abused Clergy Wife's Message to the Church: I Am Still Struggling to Survive." https:// www.abc.net.au/news/2018-10-22/what-i-want-the-church-to-know-about-domestic-violence-victims/10401752.

Alsdurf, James, and Phyllis Alsdurf. *Battered into Submission: The Tragedy of Wife Abuse in the Christian Home*. Surrey: Highland, 1989.

Annis, Ann W., and Rodger R. Rice. "A Survey of Abuse Prevalence in the Christian Reformed Church." *Journal of Religion and Abuse* 3 (2001) 7–14.

Anglican Diocese of Sydney. "Responding to Domestic Abuse: Provisional Policy and Good Practice Guidelines." https://safeministry.org.au/wp-content/uploads/2017/11/Responding-to-Domestic-Abuse.Policy-And-Guidelines.Synod2017.full-resources.pdf.

Arnold, Clinton E. *Ephesians*. Grand Rapids: Zondervan, 2010.

Aune, Kristin, and Rebecca Barnes. *In Churches Too: Church's Response to Domestic Abuse: A Case Study in Cambia*. Churches Together in Cambria, 2018. https://restored. contentfiles.net/media/resources/files/churches_web.pdf.

"Australian Churches Risk Becoming a Haven for Abusers." https://www.abc.net.au/news/2017-07-21/australia-church-risks-becoming-haven-for-abusers/8651318.

Australian Institute of Health and Welfare. "Family, Domestic and Sexual Violence in Australia." https://www.aihw.gov.au/getmedia/d1a8d479-a39a-48c1-bbe2-4b27c7 a321e0/aihw-fdv-02.pdf.aspx?inline=true.

Bala, Nicholas. "An Historical Perspective on Family Violence and Child Abuse." *Journal of Family Studies* 14 (2007) 271–78.

Baird, Julia. "After Years of Debate Sydney Anglicans Vote for Change." https://www.smh. com.au/national/nsw/after-decades-of-debate-sydney-anglicans-vote-for-change-on-marriage-20181026-p50c74.html.

Baird, Julia, and Hayley Gleeson. "Abuse Inside Christian Marriages. Shattering the Silence: Australians Tell Their Stories of Surviving Domestic Violence in the Church." https://www.abc.net.au/news/2017-08-18/shattering-silence-surviving-domestic-violence-in-church/8788902.

———. "Domestic Violence in the Church." https://www.abc.net.au/news/2018-05-23/when-women-are-believed-the-church-will-change/9782184.

———. "Submit to Your Husbands." https://www.google.com/search?q=baird+and+gleeson%2C+submit+to+your+husbands&rlz=1C1CHBF_en-GBAU813AU813&oq=baird+and+gleeson%2C+submit+to+your+husbands&aqs=chrome..69i57.15633j0j8&sourceid=chrome&ie=UTF-8.

Baker, Lynne. *Counselling Christian Women: On How to Deal with Domestic Abuse*. Bowen Hills, Qld: Australian Academic Press, 2010.

Bancroft, Lundy. *When Dad Hurts Mum: Helping Children Heal the Wounds of Witnessing Abuse*, New York: Berkley, 2004.

———. *Why Does He Do That: Inside the Minds of Angry and Controlling Men*. New York: Berkley, 2002.

Barr, Beth Alison. "Will Beth Moore Help Save Evangelicalism?" https://www.patheos.com/blogs/anxiousbench/2018/04/beth-moore-could-turn-the-tide-against-traditional-gender-roles-within-the-evangelical-church/.

Beck, James, and Kroeger, Catherine Clark. *Abuse and the Bible: How Scripture Can be Used to Hurt and to Heal*. Grand Rapids: Baker, 1996.

———. *Healing and Hurting: Giving Hope and Help to Abused Women*. Grand Rapids: Baker, 1998.

"Bodies of Liberties, 1641." https://thehistoricpresent.com/tag/1641-body-of-liberties/.

Boorstein, Michelle, and Pulliam Sarah. "Women Led to the Dramatic Rise and Fall of Southern Baptist Leader, Paige Patterson." June 11, 2018. https://www.washingtonpost.com/local/social-issues/how-women-led-to-the-dramatic-rise-and-fall-of-southern-baptist-leader-paige-patterson/2018/06/10/eacae5a4-6a61-11e8-9e38-24e693b38637_story.html.

Bowker, Lee H. "Religious Victims and Their Religious Leaders: Services Delivered to One Thousand Battered Women by the Clergy." In *Abuse and Religion: When Praying Isn't Enough*, edited by Anne L. Horton and Judith A. Williamson, 229–34. Lexington, MA: Lexington, 1988.

"British Women's Emancipation since the Renaissance." http://www.historyofwomen.org/.

Brown, Rachel. "Sydney Anglican Church Addresses Domestic Abuse." *Sydney Morning Herald*, June 5, 2015. https://www.smh.com.au/national/nsw/sydney-anglican-church-addresses-domestic-violence-20150605-ghhrzx.html.

Burgess, Katherine. "Debate Over Women's Roles Breaks Out on the Eve of Southern Baptist Meeting." https://www.commercialappeal.com/story/news/2019/06/09/southern-baptist-convention-beth-moore-sparks-debate/1332128001/.

Burk, Denny. "Complementarianism or Patriarchy? What's in a Name?" http://www.dennyburk.com/complementarianism-or-patriarchy-whats-in-a-name/.

Carlson, Bonnie, E. "Causes and Maintenance of Domestic Abuse." https://www.jstor.org/stable/30011762?seq=1#metadata_info_tab_contents.

Carter, Jimmy. *A Call to Action: Women, Religion, Violence and Power*. New York: Simon and Shuster, 2014.

Carter, Joe. "Debatable: Is Complementarianism Another Word for Patriarchy?" https://www.thegospelcoalition.org/article/debatable-is-complementarianism-another-word-for-patriarchy/.

———. "The FAQs: Southern Baptists Release Urgent Report on Sexual Abuse." https://www.thegospelcoalition.org/article/faqs-southern-baptist-release-critical-report-sexual-abuse/.

Cervin, Richard S. "On the Significance of *Kephalē* (Head)." *Priscilla Papers* 30 (2016) 8–10.

"Change the Story." https://www.ourwatch.org.au/getmedia/0aa0109b-6b03-43f2-85fe-a9f5ec92ae4e/Change-the-story-framework-prevent-violence-women-children-AA-new.pdf.aspx.

Church of England. "Responding Well to Domestic Abuse." https://www.churchofengland.org/sites/default/files/2017-11/responding-well-to-domestic-abuse-formatted-master-copy-030317.pdf.

Cole, Stephen J. "Living With a Difficult Husband." https://bible.org/seriespage/lesson-14-living-difficult-husband-1-peter-31-6.

"Definitions of Domestic Violence: Literature Review." https://www.ukessays.com/essays/criminology/literature-review-domestic-violence.php.

Dill, Russell Pepper. *A Rhetorical Analysis of Selective Pro-Slavery Sermons by Presbyterian Clergy in the Antebellum South.* PhD thesis, Louisiana State University, 1994. https://digitalcommons.lsu.edu/cgi/viewcontent.cgi?article=6722&context=gradschool_disstheses.

"Domestic Abuse—The Methodist Church." https://www.methodist.org.uk/about-us/the-methodist-church/views-of-the-church/domestic-abuse/.

"Domestic Violence in Australia." Australia's National Research Organization for Women's Safety (ANROW).

"Domestic Violence Definition." https://www.whiteribbon.org.au/understand-domestic-violence/what-is-domestic-violence/domestic-violence-definition/.

"Domestic Violence Statistics." http://hoperisingtx.org/about/domestic-violence-statistics/.

Dutton, Donald, with Susan Galant. *The Batterer: A Psychological Profile.* New York: Basic Books, 1997.

Enzell, Cynthia. "Power, Patriarchy, and Abusive Marriages." In *Healing and Hurting: Giving Hope and Help to Abused Women*, edited by James Beck and Catherine Clark Kroeger, 15–40. Grand Rapids: Baker, 1998.

"Epidemiology of Domestic Violence." https://en.wikipedia.org/wiki/Epidemiology_of_domestic_violence.

"Equal but Different." http://equalbutdifferent.org/what-we-believe.

"Equal but Different. Promoting Biblical Relationships for Women and Men." Sydney. http://equalbutdifferent.org/.

"Facts and Figures: Ending Violence Against women." https://www.unwomen.org/en/what-we-do/ending-violence-against-women/facts-and-figures.

Giles, Kevin. *Patterns of Ministry Among the First Christians.* Eugene, OR: Cascade, 2017.

———. *The Rise and Fall of the Complementarian Doctrine of the Trinity.* Eugene, OR: Cascade, 2017.

———. *The Trinity and Subordinationism: The Doctrine of God and the Contemporary Gender Debate.* Downers Grove: IVP, 2002.

———. *What the Bible Actually Teaches on Women.* Eugene, OR: Cascade, 2018.

Gjelten, Tom. "Southern Baptists to Confront Sexual Abuse and the Role of Women in the Church." *NPR*, June 10, 2019. https://www.npr.org/2019/06/10/731405246/southern-baptists-to-confront-sexual-abuse-and-the-role-of-women-in-the-church.

Gleeson, Hayley. "Australian Churches Risk Becoming a Haven for Abusers." https://www.abc.net.au/news/2017-07-21/australia-church-risks-becoming-haven-for-abusers/8651318.

———. "Church Confesses to Domestic Violence in its Ranks." https://www.abc. net.au/news/2017-10-10/sydney-anglican-church-to-unveil-domestic-abuse-policy/9033426.

Gleeson, Hayley, and Julia Baird. "Anglican Diocese of Sydney Makes an Apology to Victims of Domestic Violence." https://www.abc.net.au/news/2017-10-11/anglican-diocese-of-sydney-apologises-to-abuse-victims/9038410.

———. "No Brainer: Sydney Anglicans Vote in Support of Allowing Domestic Violence Survivors to Remarry." https://www.abc.net.au/news/2018-10-24/sydney-anglicans-support-allowing-dv-survivors-divorce-remarry/10425230.

Grinwold, Eliza. "Silence is Not Spiritual: The Evangelical MeToo movement." *The New Yorker*, June 15, 2019. https://www.newyorker.com/news/on-religion/silence-is-not-spiritual-the-evangelical-metoo-movement.

Grudem, Wayne. *Evangelical Feminism and Biblical Truth*. Sisters, OR: Multnomah, 2004.

———. "The Myth of Mutual Submission as an Interpretation of Ephesians 5:21." https://cbmw.org/uncategorized/the-myth-of-mutual-submission-as-an-interp retation-of-ephesians-21/?option=com_content&task=category&sectionid=11&id =68&Itemid=12.

———. "Wives Like Sarah, And the Husbands that Honor Them: 1 Peter 3:1–7." In *Recovering Biblical Manhood and Womanhood: A Response to Evangelical Feminism*, edited by John Piper and Wayne Grudem, 194–208. Wheaton, IL: Crossway, 1991.

Hartley, Kara. "Addressing Domestic Abuse." *Essentials* (Autumn 2019) 3–4.

———. "The Evolution of the Gender Debate." *Essentials* (Winter 2019) 3–7.

Heise, L., and A. Kotsadam. "Cross-National and Multilevel Correlatives of Partner Violence: An Analysis of Data from Population-Based Surveys." *The Lancet* 3 (2015) 332–40.

Hill, Jess. "The Costs and Causes of Domestic Violence." https://www.themonthly.com.au/ issue/2015/march/1425128400/jess-hill/home-truths."

———. *See What You Made Me Do: Power, Control and Domestic Abuse*. Carlton, Victoria: Black, 2019.

"Hope Rising, Domestic Violence Statistics." http://hoperisingtx.org/about/domestic-violence-statistics/.

Instone Brewer, David. *Divorce and Remarriage in the Bible*. Grand Rapids: Eerdmans, 2002.

Jensen, Michael. *Sydney Anglicanism: An Apology*. Eugene, OR: Wipf & Stock, 2012.

John Paul II. *Mulierus Dignitatem: On the Dignity and Vocation of Women*. Homebush, NSW: St Pauls, 1988.

Keener, Craig. *. . . And Marries Another: Divorce and Remarriage in the New Testament*. Peabody, MA: Hendrickson, 2002.

Knight, George W. "Husbands and Wives as Analogues of Christ and the Church, Ephesians 5:21-33 and Colossians 3:18-19." In *Recovering Biblical Manhood and Womanhood*, edited by J. Piper and W. Grudem, 167–68. Wheaton, IL: Crossway,1991.

Knoll, Mark. *The Civil War as a Theological Crisis*. Chapel Hill, NC: University of North Carolina, 2006.

Köstenberger, Andreas, and Margaret Köstenberger. *God's Design for Man and Woman*, Wheaton, IL: Crossway, 2014.

Kristof, Nicholas, and Sheryl WuDunn. *Half the Sky: Turning Oppression into Opportunity for Women Worldwide*. New York: A. Knopf, 2009.

Kroeger, Catherine C., and James Beck. *Women Abuse and the Bible: How Scripture Can be Used to Hurt and to Heal.* Grand Rapids: Baker, 1996.

Kroeger, Catherine C., and Nancy Nason-Clark. *No Place for Abuse: Biblical and Practical Resources to Counteract Domestic Abuse.* Downers Grove, IL: InterVarsity, 2001.

Lowik, Vicki, and Annabel Taylor. "Evangelical Churches Believe Men Should Control Women: This is Why They Breed Domestic Abuse." *The Conversation,* December 9, 2019. https://theconversation.com/evangelical-churches-believe-men-should-control-women-thats-why-they-breed-domestic-violence-127437.

Manjoo, Rashid. "Violence Against Women in the United States." https://now.org/resource/violence-against-women-in-the-united-states-statistic/iolence.

"Marital Rape in the United States." *Wikipedia.* https://en.wikipedia.org/wiki/Marital_rape_in_the_United_States.

Marshall, I. Howard. "Mutual Love and Submission, Colossians 3:18-19, Ephesians 5:21-33." In *Discovering Biblical Equality: Complementarity without Hierarchy,* edited by Ronald W. Pierce and Rebecca M. Groothuis, 186–204. Downers Grove, IL: InterVarsity, 2005.

McAlister, Melani. "How Beth Moore is Helping Change the Face of Evangelical Leadership." *The Washington Post,* June 22, 2018. https://www.washingtonpost.com/news/post-nation/wp/2018/06/22/beth-moore-is-challenging-and-helping-to-change-the-face-of-evangelical-leadership/.

Merritt, Jonathan. "Southern Baptist Mid-Life Crisis." *The Atlantic,* June 10, 2019. https://www.theatlantic.com/ideas/archive/2019/06/southern-baptist-church-needs-change/591331/.

Miles, Al. *Domestic Violence: What Every Pastor Needs to Know.* Minneapolis: Fortress, 2000.

Mohler, Albert. "Debate Over Women's Roles." https://www.commercialappeal.com/story/news/2019/06/09/southern-baptist-convention-beth-moore-sparks-debate/1332128001/.

Moon, Sarah. "Some Humans are More Equal than Others; John Piper on Spousal Abuse and Submission." January 11, 2013. http://www.patheos.com/blogs/sarahoverthemoon/2013/01/some-humans-are-more-equal-than-others-john-piper-abuse-submission/.

Moore, Beth. "An Open Letter to My Brothers." May 3, 2018. https://blog.lproof.org/2018/05/a-letter-to-my-brothers.html.

Moore, Russell D. "After Patriarchy, What? Why Egalitarians are Winning the Gender Debate." *Journal of the Evangelical Society* 49 (2006) 569–76.

Moss, Danni. "Paige Patterson's Views on Domestic Violence." June 30, 2018. https://dannimoss.wordpress.com/clergy-abuse-links/abuse-in-the-church/paige-pattersons-views-on-domestic-violence/.

Mowczko, Marg. "God on Divorce (Mal 2:16)." https://margmowczko.com/divorce-malachi-2/.

Narayan, Deepa. "India's Abuse of Women is the Biggest Human Rights Violation on Earth." *The Guardian,* 2018. https://www.theguardian.com/commentisfree/2018/apr/27/india-abuse-women-human-rights-rape-girls.

Nason-Clark, Nancy. *The Battered Wife: How Christians Confront Family Violence.* Louisville, KY: Westminster, 1997.

Nason-Clark, Nancy, and Catherine Clark Kroeger. *Refuge from Abuse: Healing and Hope for Abused Christian Women.* Downers Grove, IL: IVP, 2004.

Nason-Clark, Nancy, et al. *Responding to Abuse in Christian Homes.* Eugene, OR: Wipf & Stock, 2011.

Nicalaou, Elaine, and Courtney Smith. "A #MeToo Timeline to Show How Far We've Come and How." https://www.refinery29.com/en-us/2018/10/212801/me-too-movement -history-timeline-year-weinstein.

North, Anna. "7 Positive Changes that Have Come from the #MeToo Movement." Xhttps://www.vox.com/identities/2019/10/4/20852639/me-too-movement-sexual-harassment-law-2019.

O'Brien, Peter. *The Letter to the Ephesians.* Leicester: Eerdmans, 1991.

Pawson, David. *Leadership is Male.* East Essex: Highland, 1988.

Payne, Philip B. *Man and Woman: One in Christ: An Exegetical and Theological Study of Paul's Letters.* Grand Rapids: Zondervan, 2009.

———. "Vaticanus Distigme-Obelos Symbols Marking Added Text, Including 1 Corinthians 14.34–5." *New Testament Studies* 63 (2017) 604–25.

Piper, John. "Does a Woman Submit to Abuse?" September, 1, 2009. www.youtube.com/ watch?v=3OkUPc2NLrM.

Priest, Naomi, and Nicholas Biddle. "The Verdict on Domestic Violence Data and the Church: Believe the Women." https://www.abc.net.au/news/2017-08-21/the-verdict-on-domestic-violence-data-and-the-church-believe/8804790.

Priscilla and Aquila Centre. https://paa.moore.edu.au/conference/.

"Rape in Marriage." *Wikipedia.* https://en.wikipedia.org/wiki/Marital_rape.

"Rape in Marriage: Australian Women's History Network." http://www.auswhn.org.au/ blog/marital-rape/.

Reeder, Caryn. "1 Peter 3:1-6: Biblical Authority and Battered Wives." *Bulletin for Biblical Research* 25 (2015) 519–39.

Reeves, Jay, and David Crary. "Southern Baptists Combat Sex Abuse." https://www. theitem.com/stories/southern-baptists-combat-sex-abuse-as-critics-rally,328755.

Roberts, Barbara. *Not Under Bondage: Biblical Divorce for Abuse, Adultery and Desertion.* Melbourne: Maschi, 2008.

Roth, Randolf. "Gender, Sex and Intimate Partner Violence in Historical Perspective." In *The Oxford Handbook of Gender, Sex and Crime,* edited by Rosemary Gartner and Bill McCatthy, 1–18. https://www.oxfordhandbooks.com/view/10.1093/ oxfordhb/9780199838707.001.0001/oxfordhb-9780199838707.

Senger, Robin. *God Hates Abuse: Abuse and the Doctrine of Headship and Submission, updated and expanded.* N.p.: Createspace, 2016.

Shellnut, Kate. "Divorce After Abuse: How Paige Patterson's Counsel Compares to other Pastors." *Christianity Today,* April 30, 2018. https://www.christianitytoday.com/ news/2018/april/paige-patterson-divorce-domestic-abuse-swbts-cbmw.html.

———. "Paige Patterson Fired by Southwestern, Stripped of Retirement Benefits." *Christianity Today,* May 30, 2018. https://www.christianitytoday.com/news/2018/ may/paige-patterson-fired-southwestern-baptist-seminary-sbc.html.

Sider, Ron. "Gender and Justice." *Priscilla Papers* 21 (2007) 1–6.

Southern Baptist Convention. "On Abuse." http://www.sbc.net/resolutions/2285/resolution-2 —on-abuse.

Smith, Claire. *God's Good Design.* N.p.: Matthias Media, 2019.

"State and Federal Domestic Violence Laws in the United States." http://www.stopvaw.org/ state_and_federal_domestic_violence_laws_in_the_united_states.

Storkey, Elaine. *Scars Across Humanity: Understanding and Overcoming Violence Against Women*. London: SPCK, 2015.

"Sydney Synod Responds to Domestic Abuse." https://sydneyanglicans.net/news/synod-responds-to-domestic-violence.

Thiselton, Anthony. *The First Epistle to the Corinthians*. Grand Rapids: Eerdmans, 2000.

Thistlewaite, Susan Brooks. "Battered Women and the Bible: From Subjection to Liberation." *Christianity and Crisis* 41 (1981) 308–13.

Tracy, Steven R. "Asking Christians To Do Better by Domestic Violence Victims is Not an Attack on Christianity." July 27, 2017. https://www.abc.net.au/news/2017-07-28/not-an-attack-on-christianity-to-call-out-domestic-violence/8751856.

———. "Clergy Responses to Domestic Advice." *Priscilla Papers* 201 (2007) 9–16.

———. *Mending the Soul: Understanding and Healing Abuse*. Grand Rapids: Zondervan, 2005.

———. "Patriarchy and Domestic Abuse: Challenging Common Misconceptions." *Journal of the Evangelical Theological Society* 50 (2007) 573–94.

Tucker, Ruth. *Black and White Bible, Black and Blue Wife My Story of Finding Hope After Domestic Abuse*. Grand Rapids: Zondervan, 2016.

"Violence Against Women in India." https://en.wikipedia.org/wiki/Violence_against_women_in_India.

"Violence Against Women in the United States." https://now.org/resource/violence-against-women-in-the-united-states-statistic/violence.

Wall, Liz. "Gender Equality and Violence Against Women." *Australian Institute of Family Studies* (2014) 1–15. https://aifs.gov.au/publications/gender-equality-and-violence-against-women.

Wilcox, Brad. "Evangelicals and Domestic Abuse. Are Christian Men More Abusive?" *Christianity Today*, December 11, 2017. https://www.christianitytoday.com/ct/2017/december-web-only/evangelicals-domestic-violence-christian-men-domestic-abuse.html.

Wojtczak, Helena. "British Women's Emancipation Since the Renaissance." www. http://www.historyofwomen.org/.

World Health Organization. "Global and Regional Estimates of Violence Against Women." https://www.who.int/reproductivehealth/publications/violence/9789241564625/en/.

———. "Violence Against Women." November 29, 2017. https://www.who.int/news-room/fact-sheets/detail/violence-against-women.

Yates, Eustacia. "Domestic Violence and Ministry Implications." https://www.corneyandlind.com.au/files/webinars/Domestic-Violence-.Ministry.pdf.

Yodanis, L. Carol. "Gender Inequality, Violence Against Women and Fear: A Cross-National Test of the Feminist Theory of Violence Against Women." *Journal of Interpersonal Violence* 19 (2004) 655–75.

Young, Isabella. "Abuse Inside Christian Marriages—a Personal Story." https://www.smh.com.au/national/abuse-inside-christian-marriages--a-personal-story-20150301-13rrvr.html.

Author and Named People Index

Subject Index

Bible Index

Printed in Great Britain
by Amazon